Logoteunison

Literary Easternization in Orhan Pamuk's Works

Saman Hashemipour
Girne American University, Turkey

Series in Literary Studies

Copyright © 2020 Vernon Press, an imprint of Vernon Art and Science Inc, on behalf of the author.

All rights reserved. No part of this publication may be reproduced, stored in a retrieval system, or transmitted in any form or by any means, electronic, mechanical, photocopying, recording, or otherwise, without the prior permission of Vernon Art and Science Inc.

www.vernonpress.com

In the Americas:
Vernon Press
1000 N West Street,
Suite 1200, Wilmington,
Delaware 19801
United States

In the rest of the world:
Vernon Press
C/Sancti Espiritu 17,
Malaga, 29006
Spain

Series in Literary Studies

Library of Congress Control Number: 2019937674

ISBN: 978-1-62273-786-4

Also available: 978-1-62273-606-5 [Hardback]; 978-1-62273-815-1 [PDF, E-Book]

Cover design by Vernon Press. Cover image by Adbar:

https://commons.wikimedia.org/wiki/File:Bosphorus_aerial_view.jpg

Product and company names mentioned in this work are the trademarks of their respective owners. While every care has been taken in preparing this work, neither the authors nor Vernon Art and Science Inc. may be held responsible for any loss or damage caused or alleged to be caused directly or indirectly by the information contained in it.

Every effort has been made to trace all copyright holders, but if any have been inadvertently overlooked the publisher will be pleased to include any necessary credits in any subsequent reprint or edition.

Table of contents

Introduction		*vii*
Chapter 1	**What is Easternization?**	1
Chapter 2	**Neo-Weberian Theory of Easternization**	9
Chapter 3	**Easternization and Sufism**	13
Chapter 4	**Easternization as the Reverse of *Orientalism***	17
Chapter 5	**Easternization of the Postmodern Age**	25
Chapter 6	**East and West in the Age of Easternization**	31
Chapter 7	**Easternization is the Other of Itself**	39
Chapter 8	**Easternization for Pamuk as a Turk**	47
Chapter 9	**Easternization of World Literature**	53
Chapter 10	**Intertextuality Represents Literary Easternization**	65
Chapter 11	**Classical Eastern Literary Masterpieces Represent Literary Easternization**	81
	11.1. Masterpieces of Eastern Romantic Literature	
	11.2. Didactic and Sufi Thematic Eastern Masterpieces	
Chapter 12	**Logoteunison: The Social Theory of Easternization Behind Literature**	99
Conclusion		*113*
References		*123*
Secondary Sources		*129*
Index		*135*

To My Lovely Parents and Sasan

Introduction

The Nobel Committee for Literature at the Swedish Academy announced Orhan Pamuk as a writer who "in the quest for the melancholic soul of his native city has discovered new symbols for the clash and interlacing of cultures."[1] Orhan Pamuk sees himself as a Turkish and local, as well as a postmodern and global author. He sees himself as both Turkish and Western—that is, "global" in present-day jargon by saying: "My world is a mixture of the local—the national—and the West"[2]. According to his personal website, Sander L. Gilman, an American literary historian, describes him as "a central figure in any understanding of the 'new' Turkey and through this understanding the desires and aims of a large swath of North Africa and [the] Middle East"[3]. In 2017, the President of Germany, Steinmeier, celebrated Orhan Pamuk's birthday and introduced him as a "great narrator, a passionate European, a critical analyst of politics and society"[4].

In an interview, Pamuk points out how he went back to his "roots" and tried to "invent a modern national literature"[5]. Although he tries to illustrate and maintain a complete cultural heritage: "we are completely devoted to the Turkish traditions that have come down over thousands of years"[6], but his novels are not in a particular historical and cultural position, they portray a global view of humanity in any nation. During his visit to Turkey in 2004, former United States President George W. Bush pointed to Orhan Pamuk's works as "a bridge between cultures." What is important, he says, is to realize "that other people in other continents and civilizations" are "exactly like you"[7].

Pamuk represents identity problems of people such as being stuck between East and West or Past and Present; thus it is understandable that a writer like Pamuk would choose one of the most significant capital cities of Ottoman Empire– a multinational, multilingual empire controlling parts of Southeast, Eastern, and Central Europe, Western Asia, the Caucasus, and North Africa— as a theme for his works. In his theoretical non-fiction, *The Naïve and the*

---

[1] Orhan Pamuk 2019, 1
[2] Pamuk 2007, 410
[3] Afridi 2012, xv
[4] Sencer 2017, 1
[5] Pamuk 2007, 366
[6] Pamuk 2012b, 210
[7] Spengler 2006, 1

Sentimental Novelist, Pamuk emphasized that after reading about any coincidence, everything that "remains" in mind is not "history", but "our thoughts on the fragility of human life, the immensity of the world, and our place in the universe; and in the course of reading, we have had the pleasure of experiencing the sentence-by-sentence illumination of a center"[8]. In the twenty-first century, when Turkey seeks international integration, Pamuk condemns both Turks because of their cultural identity crisis, and also Europeans for biased denunciation of Turkish culture: "I will remain all alone with my pains, my past, and my thoughts. All right, leave me to my nice thoughts"[9]. This is a fantasy that the main character of Pamuk's screenplay *The Hidden Face* experiences; he imagines the world as a different landscape.

Studying at İstanbul's American Robert College, a branch of the American Ivy League, Pamuk knows how to write to be accepted as a new global author by a Western reader. His challenge is to be a respected author and a famous novelist at the same time. In chapter fifty-six of *Other Colours*, Pamuk points out the importance of novels in the national art of previous centuries, as he recalls its effects on international literary views today. He reviews the latest decades and their cultural order by screening recent literary authors as writers who "gradually write less for their own national majorities (who do not read them) than for the small minority of literary readers in the world who do"[10]. Pamuk, on the other hand, seeks "to engage with the world in which he lives…to understand his changing position in the world"[11].

Azade Seyhan in her book about the modern Turkish novel states that Pamuk's international success increased public interest in Turkish authors' translated works. She emphasizes that this matter leads to "a closer investigation of the cultural spaces from which modern Turkish literature has drawn intellectual and aesthetic substance"[12]. These widely disparate views about his works are because of the different perspectives of readers on the same texts. Perceptions and associations in Pamuk's works foster a global perspective of humankind despite settings in specific cultures and periods. He combines literature and social history and sometimes changes some historical facts intentionally to challenge historical perceptions. Pamuk even uses his family to explain the pros and cons of his times: alienation, isolation,

---

[8] Pamuk 2011b, 163
[9] Pamuk 2012b, 95
[10] Pamuk 2007, 243
[11] *Ibid.*
[12] Seyhan 2008, 4

industrialization, the effects of Eastern history on the West, and Western ideas on the development of the East.

As Turkey's best-selling international author who sold over eleven million copies of his books in over sixty languages, Pamuk's writing style is compared to Kafka, Gabriel Garcia Marquez, and Paul Auster. All of Pamuk's works, except for his first novel and his only screenplay, have been translated into more than fifty languages. Local feelings in Turkey are conflicted about Pamuk and his works. Some even say that Pamuk is not that good a writer and that what he says seems amusing in other languages while it is dark and dull in Turkish. However, Pamuk as an author and philosopher deals with the difficulties and problems that Turks face in a modern state while trying to discover their cultural roots. Loss of identity in an era of globalization makes him an important figure in Turkish society that is trying to be born from its ashes.

Turkish literature is comprised of both oral and written texts, either in less perfect literary forms (such as that of oral folk literature in the Republic of Turkey today), or in its previous, highly stylized Ottoman forms that are the basis of much of the written core that was influenced by Arabic and Persian language and literature, and that used the Ottoman Turkish alphabet in Arabic and Persian script. Turkish literature's inheritance of written works extends back twelve centuries under the influence of Persian and Arabic poetry. Intellectuals absorbed Arabic and Persian vocabulary and grammatical rules, forms, rhyme, meter, rhythm patterns, mythology and the *Weltanschauung* of these two languages and cultures. As the Turks embraced Islam, they showed a passion for Islamic narrative traditions in Arabic and Persian, and also the richly Persian literature of countless new tales.

My Name is Red, and *The Black Book* are two of Pamuk's prominent novels concerned with Turkish identity and introduce Turkish Divan poets with their homoerotic fantasies and early Western travellers' tales. *My Name is Red* is about the Westernization of Ottoman visual art of the Persian tradition of miniature painting, which had been protected by the Sultans during the sixteenth century. On the other hand, *The Black Book* analyzes the identity of the Turkish people and Istanbul's identity as a city between East and West, antiquity and modern secularism, and Islam. It judges modern time through the loss and gains of the collective culture. Pamuk considers the relation of personal and group identity to morals and ethics, and links between identity and culture.

Ferdowsi, Nizami, and Saadi are some of the Eastern, Persian poets praised in Pamuk's novels. Luculently, Pamuk describes how the texts of the past make the present. References to the mystic Sufi tradition of the East against the West show how Pamuk tries to keep Eastern values alive. The academy that awarded the Nobel Prize in Literature to Pamuk mentioned him as a writer who found signs and symbols of the clash of cultures in his native Istanbul, as the symbols of his country. Like the miniaturists in *My Name is Red*, the central characters of *The Black Book* convey what they meant in pieces of the past.

In this regard, Shams al-Din of Tabriz was the most influential person in Rumi's life, and after a year or two they remained inseparable in Rumi's house, and Rumi became a different man. *Diwan*-i Shams al-Din of Tabriz and the story of Rumi and Shams is one of the need-to-know parts of *The Black Book*. Also in *The Black Book* Pamuk cites the mystical parable, *The Parliament of Birds* by Attar, a poem that shows the author in his role of allegorist. The fantastic adventure of *One Thousand and One Nights* or the book known in English as the *Arabian Nights*, which reminds the readers of ancient Persian civilization, is another important masterpiece cited in Pamuk's work. These collected folk tales by various authors is a heritage of centuries. The ruler's wife Scheherazade begins to tell the king Shahryar a tale that does not end. The king, who is interested in how the story ends, postpones his wife's execution in order to hear the finale.

My Name is Red and its main character Kara make allusions to Nizami's *Khusrau and Shirin* and also, *Laila and Majnun*. *Khusrau and Shirin* recounts couplets of the love story of the Sassanian emperor, Khausrau Parviz and his beloved Shirin, and the tragedy of his rival, poor Farhad. Also, *Laila and Majnun* is the melancholic passion of the desert-poet Qais or Majnun for the lovely Laila. Jami's *Yusuf and Zulaikha*, which was written on the same subject, is another book referred to Pamuk's work. Jami's work points to the story of the prophet Joseph and Potiphar's wife as told in the surah Joseph of *The Holy Quran*.

The Epic of Kings or *Shahnameh* by Ferdowsi is the national epic of Iran and the Persian speaking countries. The work is regarded as a literary masterpiece of poetry and historiography. *Shahnameh*'s stories of fighting the injustice optimized at the battle of the father (Rostam) and the son (Esfandiyar) is not only mentioned in *My Name is Red*, but also in Pamuk's other novels, too. The great Persian poet, Saadi, whose *Bustan*, which means "the fruit orchard," contains Saadi's long experience and his judgments upon life. *Kalila and Dimna*, a collection of humorous stories about animals, and also Jami's *Haft Awrang*, meaning "Seven Thrones," are other Persian masterpieces that appear in Pamuk's *My Name is Red*. The story of the great Persian mystics, revolutionary writers, the theoretician of Sufism, hagiographers, and teachers of Sufism like Mansur Hallaj, Attar, Shams al-Din of Tabriz, and Bukhari in *The Black Book* and other mystics, writers, and preachers like Ahmad Ghazali and Muhammad Ghazali in *My Name is Red*, show influential and adaptable aspects of Persian literature. These are some of the Eastern classical literary treasures that Pamuk uses to introduce Eastern values.

Introduction

This study consists of four chapters. Chapter one deals with the theoretical background of the research and includes two topics: "Easternization" includes eight parts: first, the theory of Easternization to demonstrate how Colin Campbell methodologically defines this cultural term is reviewed. Second, Max Weber's sociological view through Campbell, as a neo-Weberian sociologist is analyzed. Third, the impact of the New Age Movement and particularly Sufism in contemporary Western countries is fully discussed. Fourth, Edward Said's theory of *Orientalism* as a theory of the East in the West and its similarities and contrasts with the Easternization thesis is mentioned. Fifth, the features of postmodernism in the age of Easternization is described. Sixth, the binary concepts of East and West, and Us and the Other is studied. Finally, the importance of Istanbul to demonstrate how this city as a bridge between East and West and a symbol to analyze the Easternization thesis is reviewed. The second topic defines a conceptual theory of "Literary Easternization." Based on the sociological theory of Easternization, a new approach of Easternization in literary study is assembled. This title includes two parts: first, through studying David Damrosch's concept of World Literature as a revised statement of comparative literature, the idea of Literary Easternization in the context of world literature is reviewed. Second, Literary Easternization in the scope of my concept of Logoteunison is explained.

In Chapter 2 the effect of intertextuality and pastiche as essential techniques in Literary Easternization to bridge genres, styles, and cultures is evaluated. Successive theories of intertextuality by Kristeva, Barthes, Bakhtin, Jenny, and Riffaterre to demonstrate how Pamuk uses intertextuality in his works are described. As Eastern masterpieces play a significant role in Pamuk's novels, the main focus of this chapter is to show how Pamuk uses intertextuality and pastiche in his books.

Chapter 1

What is Easternization?

The term "Easternization" was first used by Raphael Kaplinsky and Anne Posthuma in *Easternization: The Spread of Japanese Management Techniques to Developing Countries* (1994). The book considers the spread of oriental management techniques to the West. It discusses the industrial strength of Japan and its developing superiority which leads Western firms. Although the book was about economic adaptations of the West from Far East countries, it now refers mainly to cultural changes. Colin Campbell, the former British Emeritus professor of Sociology at York University, used the term to explain that Western civilization has been deeply affected by ideas derived from Asia. He published *Easternization of the West: A Thematic Account of Cultural Change in the Modern Era* (2008), which became the second and the last book published under the "Easternization" title to define this gradient until now. The suffix "-ization" as the last syllables of the term "Easternization," means "make, convert, or give new characteristics" and the suffix "-ize" which is added to adjectives and nouns, shows a change in behaviour, process, or conditions. In the preface, Campbell describes *Easternization of the West* as a work to show "changing beliefs and values" and a shred of evidence "to the history of the penetration of the West by Eastern forms of thought"[1]. Like the former book by Kaplinsky and Posthuma, Campbell studies changes in the West since the end of World War II—but in the cultural field.

Campbell is a neo-Weberian critic, and neo-Weberians are European modernizers whose works relate to differences in life chances in the class positions of individuals, based on Max Weber's concepts of class and status. German philosopher, Max Weber, conceived the idea of subcultures—groups with certain values, lifestyles, ethnicities, religions, and regions within a culture. Weber also explains that people use symbols to express their worldviews. The concept of worldview originates from the German word *Weltanschauung*, which refers to a socio-cultural interpretation and interaction with the world. Worldviews reflect a global concept of cultures to make sense of the world. Campbell defines Easternization or "East in the West"[2] as a worldview that

---

[1] Campbell 2008, viii
[2] *Ibid.*, 15

relates to people's behaviour and beliefs, based on Weber's concept of culture. Weber in *Sociology of Religion* mentions mankind's attempt to conceive the world as an ordered "meaningful" "cosmos" to express their cultural beliefs. Social scientists and especially positivists before Max Weber believed social matters evolve as the result of the internal movement, without the involvement of humanity. In contrast, Weber concentrated on social action that objectively considers human life in society. He saw social growth as a result of people's intent, developed in understanding and intentions over time. Weber tries to understand the meaning of social behaviour. The realization for Weber is the meaning of an act or a social relationship, and he seeks to follow the course of response action in human, which he calls sympathy or empathy. It is a reality that must be considered through the perspective of individual self-study, not from the standpoint of the researcher.

Campbell believes that the self-Easternization of the West does not happen by force. He emphasizes that the beliefs and values characterized by the West are not necessarily Eastern in nature and their birthplace is not necessarily Asia. Easternization refers to an ideal worldview that is arbitrary for both East and West. In addition, Easternization is not promulgated within Eastern civilization and does not claim that nothing remains of Western civilization and its worldview. Campbell asserts that "all that the Easternization thesis involves is the claim that what was formerly the major component of Western civilization now occupies a minority position"[3]. During the height of the colonial era, Western missionaries "acted as the primary agents of Westernization"[4] to impose their values systematically on the East. The system was reversed with interest in Eastern spiritual wisdom in the late eighteenth century—the Age of Enlightenment in Western intellectual history—whereby the West became open to the spiritual teachings of the East and was developed by writers, intellectuals, and artists. Campbell describes how the gradual import of Eastern values Easternized the West based on the open, secular values of Westerners. This cultural adaptation of what was originally an Eastern worldview by the West is defined as "Easternization." Briefly, Easternization identifies any Eastern worldviews that "exist within the civilization of the West"[5]. Although Easternization is "a process of de-Westernization"[6], for Campbell, it is also the influence of the East over the culture of the West and the West's image of the East, without accepting any domination over Western culture.

---

[3] *Ibid.*, 363
[4] *Ibid.*, 23
[5] *Ibid.*, 39
[6] *Ibid.*, 41

Campbell describes Easternization of the West as a process that, although the West is not colonized by the East, the East influences Western values, beliefs, or briefly their worldview. The process of Easternization is the Easternization of an individual Western citizen's thought and view. In 1942 Howard Wilson, a professor at the Harvard Graduate School of Education and the editor of the *Harvard Educational Review*, used the "easternization of America" to define what he called "the 'glib' talk for years about the 'westernization of Asia'"[7]. Campbell finds culture a kind of overarching system of worldviews rather than a compilation of behaviour and meaning.

Through Weber's *Sociology of Religion*, Campbell constructs two ideal types of religious and cultural orientations. The "Eastern" religious orientation concentrates on an immanent divinity of souls in the highest level of the eternal divine principle. The "Western" mode, represented by Judaism, Christianity, and Islam, suggests a personal god whose power is beyond the world and its creatures. For Campbell, both religious and cultural orientations are logical and not empirically derived. Thus, although for Campbell there were always elements of "East in the West" as well as the "West in the East," he states that these are ideal-typical religious orientations in the Weberian senses that not any religion or civilization can par directly with either. Besides, any civilization or, the religious and philosophical cultural complex should be a mixture of the two types[8]. Campbell's main argument is that an entirely secular and scientific worldview turned to the East because there was no other alternative.

Ever-continuing tension between the local and universal is a familiar topic for humanities researchers who have debated this topic for years. The majority of thinkers believe that the "global" perspectives of today follow a hegemonic Eurocentric cultural vision that assesses other cultures based on its own values. Thus, the assimilative nature of global perspectives in cultural discourse is up for debate. The Sociologist, Bryan Turner reminds us that sociology suggests we cannot choose modernization, for instance, without its cultural system of thought. For example, we cannot judge the Islamization of knowledge if our knowledge is modernist or anti-modernist. He says the world religions have always claimed to be global, but the important point is the processes of globalization and understanding the concept of the world from the perspective of different cultures. Considering Islam within a problematic relationship to rationalist modernity and to the Christian West is a kind of Occidentalism as a reaction among Asian and African scholars against Orientalism or against the global civilization imposed by the West. Moreover, making a distinction between

---

[7] Shaffer 2001, 9
[8] Campbell 2008, 175

high and low culture is part of the process of globalization. Homi Bhabha thinks that globalization "must always begin at home"[9]. He affirms that globalization's progress is measured by "how globalizing nations deal with 'the difference within'"[10] and how this "imagined community" solves the problems of diversity and minority rights. Globalization raises the possibility that all cultural systems are local cultures because it is difficult to sustain the idea; for example, that British culture is a global culture. Reflexivity and cultural propinquity in a global context also produce a new focus on the self in postmodernity, because the relationship between individual and national identity becomes highly unstable and uncertain[11]. For Campbell, globalization has the same meaning as Westernization because cultural globalization is influenced by Western movements happening in the West.

Hannah Arendt thinks that some communities are judged by other organized communities in the new global political organization because "there was no longer any uncivilized spot on earth" and also people live in "One World"[12]. Global cosmopolitanism finds the world as global communities that consist of national societies. Globalization challenged much of the traditional dominant cultures of nation-states, represented by multiculturalism. Nation-states have to investigate the character of their national cultural identities. Globalization results in a variety of traditions within a community and produces a new level of cultural diversity and multiculturalism. Multiculturalism, which is derived from the European Enlightenment, led hermeneutics to see even scriptural texts as secular classical texts. It describes the establishment of multiple cultural traditions within a single one and judges equally in terms of cultures associated with ethnic groups. This judgement is one of a variety of different positions. Besides, "cosmopolitan" means "citizen of the cosmos," which takes a sceptical view toward local customs and traditions. This definition is similar to the Weberian worldview used by Campbell in defining Easternization.

Appiah refers to cosmopolitanism as the universe and not just the earth. He adds that cosmopolitanism as a study initially rejects "the conventional view that every civilized person belong[s] to a community among communities"[13]. Based on Appiah's ideas, two fields interlock in defining the cosmopolitan concept: first, we have obligations to others based on citizenship. Second, we can learn much from human differences in the lifestyles of different societies.

---

[9] Bhabha 1994, xv
[10] *Ibid.*, xv
[11] Turner 1994, 184
[12] Arendt 1973, 297
[13] Appiah 2006, xiv

These two ideals assume a universal concern about each other and respect for each other. Therefore, cosmopolitanism is a solution to the conflict. Appiah thinks defining cosmopolitanism is worrying because you need to define a universal term with its local responsibilities. The confusing term in this process is "nationalism," because "If national allegiances are reasons for actions, they will sometimes interfere with the reasons presented by more local, and 'thicker,' allegiances"[14]. Campbell's Easternization looks more realistic than cosmopolitan society because Easternization is based on evidence, but cosmopolitanism is based on an imagined world of equal rights.

Former Iranian president Mohammad Khatami introduced the idea of "Dialogue Among Civilizations" as a response to Samuel P. Huntington's theory of a "Clash of Civilizations." In November 1998, the General Assembly of the United Nations proclaimed the year 2001 as the "United Nations Year of Dialogue among Civilizations" or, as Todorov calls it, a "dialogue between civilizations"[15]. Aimé Césaire admits a contact of different civilizations, and that is because "for civilizations, exchange is oxygen"[16]. He believed Europe was lucky since there were "crossroads" because it was "the locus of all ideas, the receptacle of all philosophies, the meeting place of all sentiments," so as a result, it was "the best center for the redistribution of energy"[17] in which "energy" meant elucidating theoretical ideas. Césaire criticizes dogmatic fans of Eurocentric views who think that "the West invented science" or "the West alone knows how to think"[18], so that consequently at "the borders of the Western world there begins the shadowy realm of primitive thinking, which, dominated by the notion of participation, incapable of logic, is the very model of faulty thinking"[19]. Césaire approves an admixture of different worlds and finds that opinionated assertions need to be colonized inside minds "at the same time that we decolonize society"[20]. Benedict Anderson says that modern Western social philosophy in its global perspective is "limited by the contingencies of global power" and "'Western universalism' no less than 'Oriental exceptionalism' can be shown to be only a particular form of a richer, more diverse, and differentiated conceptualization of a new universal idea"[21]. Likewise, Hans-Georg Gadamer describes "a global uniformity which

---

[14] Appiah 2007, 239
[15] Todorov 2010, 165
[16] Césaire 2000, 33
[17] *Ibid.*
[18] *Ibid.*, 69
[19] *Ibid.*
[20] Césaire 2000, 94
[21] Anderson 2012, 224

is 'unity in diversity'"[22]. He says humanity should "appreciate and tolerate pluralities, multiplicities, cultural differences"[23]. He warns that the hegemony or "unchallengeable power of any one single nation" is "dangerous for humanity because it goes "against human freedom"[24]. He finds this concept as "the heritage of Europe"[25]. Such unity in diversity should be universally extended because "every culture, every people has something distinctive to offer for the solidarity and welfare of humanity"[26].

According to Campbell, globalization is the process of international integration of worldviews and cultures. One of the phases in the history of globalization is Archaic globalization, which refers to globalizing the earliest civilizations until the seventeenth century. Early modern globalization spans two centuries and is followed by so-called Modern globalization in the nineteenth century. The history of globalization shows that without the traditional ideas from the East, Western globalization would not have occurred as it did. Campbell says that the concept of globalization that was established in the 1970s is just "another name for Westernization"[27]. He discusses how arguments over cultural globalization occur within the context of Western values and events in the West by telling that Westernization is occurring everywhere; consequently, the West got "apotheosis of Westernness," that culturally will remain unchanged anymore, or the West becomes "even more intensively Western that it is at present."[28] He says even if academics believe that countries all around the world are gradually adopting the West, there "exists certain blindness" about anything different may happen in the West.[29]

Demonstrating any discourse outside of its own borders is impossible. To reach this aim, a thesis should be tested in readers' thoughts. If needed, the Easternization thesis should be studied outside of European borders, in a place that links East and West to define such a global term. Istanbul is an ideal site to consider the binding of the East (Asia) and West (Europe). It is the city where East meets West. The Bosphorus bridges join two continents, and Istanbul as a whole is a mixture of Eastern and Western cultures. However, Orhan Pamuk has written in Turkish about Turkish issues and Turkey's rich literary heritage as the

---

[22] Pantham 1992, 132
[23] *Ibid.*
[24] *Ibid.*
[25] *Ibid.*
[26] *Ibid.*
[27] Campbell 2008, 18
[28] *Ibid.*, 19
[29] *Ibid.*

country where traditional and modern, religious and the secular, and East and West live together and are compatible. In Pamuk's works, Istanbul is a multi-factor, chaotic, undefinable theme with a complex identity that is an Eastern zone as much as a Western zone. Pamuk tries to define this complicated mixture of identities in Istanbul through texts and intertextuality.

Some Turkish authors have selected Istanbul as a leitmotif of their works. Ahmet Hamdi Tanpınar, Ahmet Ümit, Elif Shafak, Refik Halit Karay, Mithat Cevdet Kuntay, Kemal Tahir, Metin Kaçan, Nedim Gürsel, Mario Levi, and Zülfü Livaneli are among them. Except for Tanpınar, Ümit, Shafak, and Livaneli, most of these author's works are not translated and therefore are inaccessible to global readers. The few translated works do not reflect any theory about the importance of the city, and just represent its scenic beauty or Constantinople's history. Pamuk's works have been translated into more than sixty languages. Thus he became an international author of world literature, as Pamuk returns to the Ottoman, cosmopolitan, multicultural, multilingual, multi-ethnic past to form a national horizon for redefining Turkishness.

Chapter 2

Neo-Weberian Theory of Easternization

Based on Max Weber's ideas, Campbell points out that despite dualism emblematizes the philosophical stance of the West, the East rejects dualism because it finds the world as a wholly "connected and self-contained cosmos"[1]. Weber believes that the dualism between the worldly and spiritual, mind and body, or consciousness and nature is maintained in the Western worldview. The Western worldview psychologically increases the desire to control nature. In contrast to the materialistic dualism of the Western worldview, the East regards nature as a world pervaded with spirituality. This attitude forms the East-West division. Campbell believes that replacement of the "traditional Western dualism by an Eastern-style metaphysical monism" means the universe is not a vast and essentially alien essence that set "over and against mankind."[2] If not, humankind has to search the cosmos directly to understand how "the far distant and the close at hand" or "the past with both the present and the future" are connected.[3]

We have to realize in advance that we cannot come to a conclusion about Western ascendancy and its considerable impact on cross-cultural understanding. One of the responsibilities of Easternization is the use of hermeneutics to solve this problem of whether people can really understand other people from foreign cultures or not—even if relativism requires that there *are* no universal criteria of rationality, truth, or morality—but our knowledge of the world is subjective, not objective. Our ideas or points of view are dependent on our interpretations, emotions, personal opinions, and judgments. We are supposed to tell that the philosophy of Friedrich Nietzsche had a significant impact in developing Weberian sociology, and his anxieties about bureaucratization and culture associated him with the process of modernization. Nietzsche's "Death of God" means that God must have been a human creation in the first place and that the religious morality of slavery would eventually die.

---

[1] Campbell 2008, 58
[2] *Ibid.*, 105
[3] *Ibid.*

Weber considers capitalism to be the product of Protestantism. By use of 'value-free sociology,' Weber asserts that sociologists should value neutrality while conducting social research. Weber's sociology was to provide a historical account of the uniqueness of the West. According to Weber, in Europe, cities became independent from the state economically and politically, but in the Orient, cities were not economic centres. Turner wrote how Weber and Marx had similar explanations about the presence of history in occidental societies and its absence in the Orient, which can be regarded as "another version of that more ancient system of accounting, namely 'oriental despotism'"[4]. Turner says that there is an accounting system in Weber's sociology of Oriental society, and Oriental society is a system of "absences" in which "the Orient simply lacks the positive ingredients of Western rationality."[5].

Any Eurocentric dominant worldview ends binary notations of "us" and "other" or the East (the Orient) and the West. Campbell refers to Weber's "Ideal (pure) Type" conception of reality, which emphasizes the subjective chaos of social reality in an anti-positivist way, and reminds us that the social sciences depend on abstract and hypothetical worldviews. In opposition to Weberian rationalism, which brings about the distinctive opposition between the irrational and the rational, East and West, or primitive and civilized, Fredric Jameson thinks that the modern rational mind is not able to comprehend forms of multiplicity. He honours French intellectual, Georges Bataille (1897–1962) for remaining in the realm of experience rather than rationalization. Easternization, also, remains in the realm of evidence rather than rationalization.

The advent of global popular Western culture or "pop culture" in postmodernity and everyday life makes it easy to define new aspects of contemporary culture. The beliefs, ideas, and values of culture emerge in artefacts. Although Easternization is an evidence-based thesis, it is supported by cultural exempla, like artefacts. As human beings, we inhabit culture, which is the product of constructed values. Anthony Appiah declares that there are two confusing uses of culture: cultural heritage, or as Appiah terms it, "cultural patrimony," which refers to artefacts based on human creativity that need a knowledge of social and historical context, are not individual concepts, and are rarely universal; and another concept of "cultural patrimony" refers to the products of a culture which belong to specific groups that are "heirs to a trans-historical identity, whose patrimony they are"[6]. Edward Said asserts that current definitions of culture are interrelated with a

---

[4] Turner 1994, 41
[5] *Ibid.*
[6] Appiah 2006, 118

sense of identity and nation. This definition results in differentiation as a process of xenophobia, which creates an attitude of "us" against "them." Said calls this definition a return to traditional perspectives on culture, which are against "liberal philosophies [of] multiculturalism and hybridity"[7]. These "'returns' have produced varieties of religious and nationalist fundamentalism"[8]. Dallmayr says, "liberalism heralded an emancipation from parochial bondage and from the fetters of social inequality" that ends up as "a new and different kind of maturity. one where freedom is willing to recognize and cultivate cultural diversity"[9].

It seems that the question of cultural difference is not acute in the contemporary period anymore. Some use culture to show the gap between "us" here and "them" there. Also, Edward Said reminds us that the continued interpretation of Western culture itself made the world take a new look at it. It was done by reading their archives after imperial division in a new way. Using the Gramscian theory of hegemony, which criticizes hegemonic culture and bourgeois common sense, new interpretations through comparative literature and cultural studies help us to "challenge the sovereign and unchallenged authority of the allegedly detached Western observer"[10]. Said describes the relationship between the West and "its dominated cultural others"[11]. He thinks if we are to understand cultural forms accurately, we have to study "the formation and meaning of Western cultural practices themselves"[12]. Bryan Turner thinks that for comparatists, culture possesses some "essential characteristics in terms of which other cultures are seen to be deficient"[13]. He states that "positive and negative attributes [are] thus established by which alien cultures can be read off and summations arrived at"[14]. Subsequently, historical positions in the analysis of culture are an important clue to the selection and arrangement of information they are obliged to interpret judiciously. If we stress cultural differences, it means that we respect the uniqueness of particular cultures. According to Homi Bhabha, cultural difference signals "new forms of meaning, and strategies of identification, through processes of negotiation where no discursive authority can be

---

[7] Said 1983, xiii
[8] *Ibid.*
[9] Dallmayr 1996, 221
[10] Said 1983, 59
[11] *Ibid.*, 230
[12] *Ibid.*
[13] Turner 1994, 37
[14] *Ibid.*

established without revealing the difference of itself"[15]. Bhabha wrote the cultural difference is not "the free play of polarities and pluralities in the homogeneous empty time of the national community."[16] He believes that cultural difference is the opponent of values and meanings "associated with cultural plenitude; it represents the process of cultural interpretation formed in the perplexity of living, in the disjunctive, liminal space of national society" and declare the difference between "representations of social life without surmounting the space of incommensurable meanings and judgements that are produced within the process of transcultural negotiation."[17] Bhabha wrote, "Cultural diversity is the recognition of pre-given cultural contents and customs; held in a time-frame of relativism" that arises "liberal notions of multiculturalism, cultural exchange or the culture of humanity."[18] Also, he interpolates that Cultural diversity is "the representation of a radical rhetoric of the separation of totalized cultures that live unsullied by the intertextuality of their historical locations, safe in the Utopianism of a mythic memory of a unique collective identity."[19] It also acts as a system of the articulation of "cultural signs" in anthropology.[20]

---

[15] Bhabha 1990, 313
[16] *Ibid.,* 312
[17] *Ibid.,* 312
[18] Bhabha 1994, 50
[19] *Ibid.*
[20] *Ibid.*

Chapter 3

Easternization and Sufism

Easternization enunciates that traditional Western values and beliefs have not disappeared, but formerly settled Eastern values gradually swapped their position. Despite this, some traditional Western values and beliefs and slowly dying metanarratives still remain in the Western worldview. Campbell indicates that significant element in this view is the nature of humanity that now "prevail in the West,"[1] and he elucidates that when these elements are taken together, they resemble an ideal-typical Eastern or Western worldview.

New Age Eastern-style worldviews show that modern science and organized religion cannot fill the gaps left behind by myth, magic, and superstition. They characterize the thoughts of ordinary people in the West within a New Age worldview. Eclecticism identifies, explains, and incorporates behaviours that are variants of Hinduism, Buddhism, and Sufism that have been imported from the East to the West. Campbell believes that the gap that is not fulfilled by modern science or organized religion is sometimes fulfilled by Eastern outlooks. As a neo-Weberian, Campbell believes the point lies in Weber's rationalization thesis of changing to more rational views. Nowadays, Westerners often believe in Eastern beliefs and practices such as karma and reincarnation, Reiki and acupuncture therapy, Zen Buddhist and Krishna Consciousness religion, the practice of yoga, meditation, and t'ai chi, feng shui home design, and fashion icons such as yin-yang. Easternization examines the development of Eastern religions such as Buddhism and Hinduism, and different types of mysticism. One kind of cultural change in the West is the Easternization process. It is a platform to address the whole world and is a reverse flow from Asia to the Western world. Easternization of Western societies takes place through the importation of new religious movements drawn from Sufism, Hinduism, and Buddhism.

For Weber, the process of separation from religious connections or secularization was a hidden intrinsic feature of Western culture. Weber thought that ethical, rational monotheism promoted a disenchantment with the world. When Western culture failed to utilize science culture and religious culture, it started a self-secularization process through rationalization. Weber's theory of

---

[1] Campbell 2008, 363

rationalization explains cultural change through rising systems of control in the West, and through arbitrary decision-making in the East, to assert that the Orient, therefore, did not develop disciplined and stable governments. Based on Weber's literal and historical claims, Campbell claims that "the impetus underlying rationalization in the West appears to exhaust itself, having given full expression to its cultural potential, the end result being a totally secular, disenchanted, scientific worldview"[2]. Accordingly, as a result, because "there is nowhere else to go,"[3] the West turns East. Bourdieu thinks that although "the technologization of the self, depersonalization of the cosmos, and metaphorization of the religious field provide evidence of certain purportedly 'Eastern' themes (e.g., impersonal cosmos, sacralized self, and non-absolute religious truth)," "developments within esoteric" and also new age movements do not "represent central characteristics formative of and active within the modern Western habitus"[4]. He thinks that they are merely offering something "substantive by way of novelty"[5] and these novelties have merely found their way into Western culture today.

In 1922, Oswald Spengler in *The Decline of the West* asserted that to know how Western Culture will be accomplished, we have to know its core and relations with history, nature, science, people, other worldviews, and events. He calls the West "metaphysically-exhausted soil"[6] . For him, the Western mind sees the world as history and does not see the world just as nature, which at one time was the only theme of philosophy. He states that Classical culture retains no conscious memory, and the oriental picture was at rest, but there was a Western model of the modern era that for the first time gave the picture of progression to history. He said the Western model "presented a self-contained antithesis, with equilibrium as its outcome and a unique divine act as its turning-point"[7]. Spengler accepted that the modern history of the world is "a limited history" of the "Eastern Meditteranean" region and "West-Central Europe"[8]. He recalled that Hegel's reference to nations did not fit into his system of history, which means every historian uses everything necessary for his purpose. He criticized Western thinkers' "unshakable truths and eternal views"[9] that incessantly find the truth for their worldview. Spengler stated that people are equally certain

---

[2] *Ibid.*, 375
[3] *Ibid.*
[4] Dawson 2006, 8
[5] *Ibid.*
[6] Spengler 1927, 5
[7] *Ibid.*, 22
[8] *Ibid.*
[9] *Ibid.*, 23

about their cultural truths, and to understand the symbolism of history we need to define a universal form of thought since at present there are no constant and universal concepts. He even criticizes Western thinkers from Kant to Schopenhauer because of their restricted schemes of culture. Western culture captures a transitional phase that represents precisely the correct condition of Western Europe. The development of Western culture did not happen during an unlimited time, but from limited, definable occurrences, "calculated from available precedents"[10]. Moreover, Anthony Appiah reminds us that *The Kasidah of Haji Abdu El-Yezdi*, written by a native of Persia and translated by Sir Richard Francis Burton in the nineteenth century, blends mystical ideas of Sufism with Darwin's evolutionary theory and other Western theories of the Victorian Period. The spread of the 1960s counterculture and the subsequent New Age Movement introduced a range of occultist, spiritual beliefs and practices that grew larger in the 1970s and afterwards the United Kingdom and in the United States. Robert Ellwood comments that Western spiritual life is divided into two camps. He says there was an assumption between both the ancient Hebrews and Greeks of the Homeric era, that "men or tribes are each separate entities living and acting in the stream of world history and dominant over nature."[11] This different orientation from that of the East, "led to the unique contributions of the Western man to world culture, and as well to certain evils of the West."[12] On the other hand, Ellwood comments, the West has known Asiatic shamanism which enjoins a man's task is "to attain to individual initiatory expansions of consciousness and awareness until he becomes mentally one with the whole cosmos."[13]

Carl Gustav Jung thinks the West's imitation of the East is a painful misunderstanding of Eastern psychology, which is an alien formation for Westerners. He thinks Western culture's problems should be solved by Westerners and says "it is really regrettable that a European launches off his nature and then follows the East and deals with its impacts"[14]. He thinks if Westerners stay faithful to their identity, they can attain equal cultural values as those that Easterners inherited in a thousand years. He says "because of the limited information of the East from the external world," Eastern cultures "achieved internal stuff"[15]. He does not find Eastern values inestimable and

---

[10] *Ibid.*, 39
[11] Ellwood 1973, 42
[12] *Ibid.*
[13] Ellwood 1973, 42-43
[14] Jung 2010, 26
[15] *Ibid.*, 74

thinks the West has utilized science, and thereby Westerners by use of their historical and scientific background will get ahead of the East through psychology. For Jung, Eastern culture destroys Western Christian values. He suggests that we find Eastern values within and through unconsciousness, not outwardly. In this case, Westerners are able to comprehend unconscious spiritual values of Easterners through Western consciousness of aspects of the Freudian system. It means based upon the Freudian Ego or I concept, Westerners are able to mediate between the unrealistic Id (Eastern unconscious values) and the real external world (Western worldview). Jung thinks that Western attitudes are extroverted, while Eastern introspective attitudes aim to capture humanity's self-aware consciousness. He thinks that the Western mind's eagerness to discover unconsciousness as a psychological reality by replacing mortal things with permanent things is a Western trait.

Campbell interrogates the New Age Movement's timing and reasons. He describes the Easternization of the West as a great "cultural revolution" in the worldview of Western civilization, whereby the passive Eastern civilization's worldview "has come to dominance in its place"[16] after the 1960s. Easternization's provenance is a civilization of the East mixed with innate Asian traditions of thought. However, the New Age Movement encourages individuals to be more narcissistic, while Eastern civilizations are more collectivist in nature. Campbell says that despite New Agers' diffuse individual power to spotlight their fate in human potential movements, it is a kind of individual self-reliance, not a mark of growing individualism. Campbell discusses the importance of packaging any tradition. For a Western New Ager, there are lots of alternatives, and an Eastern worldview from Asian civilization is one of them. If Easterners tend to send their traditions to Westerners, they need to develop their traditional framework in a way to evoke more interest in new followers. Campbell thinks genuine Western-Easterners market it under the New Age Movement. By repairing defects and updating thoughts, New Agers establish a culture that can be diverted into many other alternatives, including dozens of traditions from which they now draw their material. Campbell reveals that gradually Western worldviews have changed from dualistic materialism to metaphysical monism. He describes the fading out of the union between Christian theology and the classical concept of salvation, and the mystical Eastern concept of self-deification spirituality. New Age-style belief shows a radical change of Western worldview in the Easternization thesis.

---

[16] Campbell 2008, 163

Chapter 4

Easternization as the Reverse of *Orientalism*

Easternization may refer either to processes in the East itself known as the Orient or to processes occurring in the West. The processes in the East relate back to Eastern and especially Asian values, while processes are occurring in the West concern cultural change, secularization, and spiritual revolution. Rather than criticizing, Easternization praises non-Western values and beliefs. Both Westernization and Easternization give way to single world culture. Over time, two apparently opposite poles as an orientation with different cultures and worldviews arrive at a common point in reaching the world. The term Easternization is in reverse relation with Edward Said's *Orientalism*. In reality, *Orientalism* is about the West, which "responded more to the culture that produced it than to its putative object"[1]. Even Said accepts that globalization gathers nations together as he says: "We are nowhere near 'the end of history,' but we are still far from free from monopolizing attitudes toward it. These have not been much good in the past and the quicker we teach ourselves to find alternatives, the better and safer [...] we are mixed in with one another in ways that most national systems of education have not dreamed of"[2]. Easternization helps Westerners to acquaint themselves with non-Western attitudes to question the validity of their judgments or their methodology and to improve its weaknesses. Thus, even if Easternization does not teach Westerners much about Easterners, it acts as an advisory to find strengths and weaknesses of their cultural worldview. Edward Said's *Orientalism* thesis enables Asians and the Islamic world to adapt their culture to all humankind, but Easternization does not inspect the historical process of the interaction of polar opposites in detail but observes a neutral view toward interaction of East and West.

Traditionally, Europe or the West has tended to approach other cultures, which is why Edward Said calls *Orientalism* "a way of coming to terms with the Orient that is based on the Orient's special place in European Western

---

[1] Said 2003a, 22
[2] Said 1983, 401

experience"[3]. As opposed to Orientalist works that study ancient civilizations to provide a concept for Arab-Islamic heritage, Easternization tries to interpret the present. It does not insist that non-Muslims cannot understand Islam or that non-Westerners cannot understand the culture of Christianity. Easternization tries to discover the realities of the present. Said in *Orientalism* thought people should study contemporary alternatives to Orientalism to answer the question of how one can study other cultures and peoples from a libertarian or nonrepressive and nonmanipulative perspective. Traditionally, non-Western cultures increasingly exaggerate the future of the world by banalizing "otherness" or "difference" between East and West, tradition and modernity, or polytheism and monotheism. Easternization tries to set Said's *Orientalism* perspective of criticizing the historical Western military and economic hegemony beside Huntington's vision of the Clash of Civilizations to make a dialogue between East and West. Bryan Turner in *Marx and the End of Orientalism* wrote that "The end of Orientalism requires a fundamental attack on the theoretical and epistemological roots of Orientalist scholarship which creates the long tradition of Oriental Despotism, mosaic societies and the 'Muslim City'"[4]. He explained that the end of Orientalism requires the end of "certain forms of Marxist thought and the creation of a new type of analysis"[5].

Easternization is also considered as a reversed cultural Post-Orientalistic (un)conscious movement in the West. A prominent difference between Post-Orientalism and Easternization is that Post-Orientalism considers political changes of the Middle-East during and after the Iranian Revolution, the Gulf War, and the period after September 11. Post-Orientalism studies American interests in the Middle East and the political terms in the reproduction of American nationalism. It addresses the United States and Middle Eastern relations, identity concepts, foreign policy, and the sense of "us" and the "foreign." Hamid Dabashi in *Post-Orientalism* used these terms to "think through Edward Said's insights and reflect on our contemporary conditions" and "to articulate the theoretical foregrounding of the power of self-representation and rebellious agency for the subaltern, the colonized, the dominated"[6]. Easternization sets out to solve the interconnection of Eastern and Western intellectual traditions. It is based on observed instances of regeneration and the creation of new identities. The question of who we are in the present and in the moment of post-Orientalism and post-occidentalism, answers the

---

[3] Said 2003a, 1
[4] Macfie 2000, 118-19
[5] *Ibid.*, 119
[6] Dabashi 2009, xi-xii

question of Easternization. Instead of conspiracy theories that Westernization brings about for Easterners, Easternization finds ways of putting things right to ensure equality. Easternization is different from Counter-Orientalism, which seeks to demythologize and therefore de-Orientalize, disorient, and counter Orientalist stereotypical practices in cultural models of history or identity.

Said confesses that *Orientalism* is not able to answer the "complex problem of knowledge and power"[7]. It is obvious that Said predicted Easternization: "Rather than the manufactured clash of civilizations, we need to concentrate on the slow working together of cultures that overlap, borrow from each other, and live together in far more interesting ways than any abridged or inauthentic mode of understanding can allow"[8].

Turner says that mere socio-global studies of cultural developments cannot survive anymore because they do not emphasize the sharp contrast between Occident and Orient, so there is "considerable intellectual merit" in the way of accepting our culture as "strange" and "characterized by a profound otherness"[9]. He explains it is necessary to "turn the anthropological gaze onto the history of our own religions and cultural practices"[10]. He asserts that the orientalist discourse explains the differences of we and them, East and West, and rationality versus irrationality and suggests an alternative to orientalism which is "a discourse of sameness" to emphasize "the continuities between various cultures."[11] Illustratively he declares that there should be "a new form of secular ecumenicalism" to regard Islamic cultures as part of a wider cultural complex that embraces both Judaism and Christianity.[12] He says, "Oriental despotism was simply Western monarchy writ large" and the crises and contradictions of contemporary orientalism are parts of a crisis of a Western society that is transferred to "a global context" and are only recognizable through a transformation of power or "political relations between Orient and Occident"[13]. Thereby, the orientalist discourse "on the absence of the civil society in Islam" reflects basic "political anxieties" of "political freedom in the West."[14] He mentions that "the problem of

---

[7] Said 2003a, 24
[8] Said 2003b, 1
[9] Turner 1994, 103
[10] *Ibid.*
[11] *Ibid.*, 102
[12] *Ibid.*
[13] *Ibid.*, 34-35
[14] *Ibid.*

Orientalism was not the Orient, but the Occident" and the Orient does not represent the East, but only seen as "a caricature of the West."[15]

Orientalist refers to the Western intellectual scholar and researcher of Islam and Oriental studies. This person studies a foreigner, socially and philologically. *Orientalism* is based on the fact that Occidentals talk about Orientals "while they neither know themselves adequately"[16] nor talk about Occidentals sanely. It as a discourse that divides the globe into Orient and Occident. Although Orientalism Orientalized the Orient, it seems that the task of Orientalism is to make Oriental culture more manageable and comprehensible. Actually, Edward Said criticizes essentialist, alienating, Orientalist cultural views. Said does not criticize Europe or the West, but only Eurocentric Western points of view. It seems that Said's main aim is to make us aware of an image of cultural Orientalism with racist assumptions for institutional academic studies in the humanities. Said mentioned, "Orientalism is a Western style for dominating, restructuring, and having authority over the Orient"[17]. Orientalism in common sense is scientific research of the Orient—its people, cultures, and languages—but Said's work is not an objective scholarly work that's completely devoted to the Orient. Said criticizes why Muslims and Arabs need to be analyzed and described according to European standards. His works are written for scholars, and he questions why scholars consider Arabs as an undifferentiated mass. It seems there is an inner conflict within *Orientalism*. Disconcertingly, Said refuses to accept that the Orient has to recognize itself. Said himself challenges the theory of *Orientalism* as he says Orientalism is "a considerable dimension of modern political-intellectual culture, and as such has less to do with the Orient than it does with 'our' world"[18]. Tetsu Nishio explains "the imagined Orient (= the imagined other) behaves as a self-defined entity in opposition to Europe (the reflected self)" and this process was intermingled with the process of "discovering self-consciousness in the modern sense in Europe," whereby "the various genres of literary fiction emerged in order for the imagined other and the reflected self to play their respective roles as controllable entities in the virtual narrative space."[19] Thoroughly, "Europe discovered her self-identity (or her self-consciousness as an identifiable autonomous civilization) in the virtual narrative space called Orientalism"

---

[15] *Ibid.*
[16] *Ibid.*, 45
[17] Said 2003a, 3
[18] *Ibid.*, 12
[19] Yamanaka 2006, 161

and finally the Orientalism that occurred in the European milieu should not be regarded as "a universal phenomenon applicable straightforwardly to other similar phenomena," but as a matchless phenomenon in modern European civilization and in the history of the humankind.[20]

Edward Said in *Orientalism* asserts that the Western imperialist societies constructed the East and the Orient based on their patronizing perceptions and fictional depictions of people living in Asia, North Africa, and the Middle East. Said's framework of "Other" examines the Orient from a perspective that is different from Western scholarship in order to get away from the stereotyped, dominant, colonialist, and Orientalist paradigms of the rational West and the irrational Other. Said asserts that "the Orient-versus-Occident opposition" was undesirable, "the less it was given credit for actually describing anything more than a fascinating history of interpretations and contesting interests"[21]. He criticizes the way Europe always emerges as superior to the Other. In the last paragraph of *Orientalism*, Said hopes his *Orientalism* will change the former "Oriental" concept. He says, "No former 'Oriental' will be comforted [...] to study new 'Orientals'—or 'Occidentals'—of his own making"[22]. Traditional Orientalists consider the Orient and Orientals as an object of study and of a different character emphasized by otherness which is definable by others. "This 'object' of study will be, as is customary, passive, nonparticipating, endowed with a 'historical' subjectivity, above all, non-active, non-autonomous, non-sovereign with regard to itself"[23]. Anouar Abdel-Maled reminds that narcissistic European writing in creating the orient started by Homer and Aeschylus through the creation of a series of stereotypical images, in which "Europe (the West, the 'self') is seen as being essentially rational, developed, humane, superior, authentic, active, creative and masculine, while the Orient (the East, the 'other') (a sort of surrogate, underground version of the West or the 'self') is seen as being irrational, aberrant, backward, crude, despotic, inferior, inauthentic, passive, feminine and sexually corrupt."[24] He thinks during the process, other 'orientalist' fantasies such as 'Arab mind,' an 'oriental psyche' and 'Islamic Society' were invented by the orientalist that ends to "the construction of a 'saturating hegemonic system,' designed, consciously or unconsciously, to dominate,

---

[20] *Ibid.*
[21] Said 2003a, 336
[22] *Ibid.*, 328
[23] Macfie 2000, 50
[24] *Ibid.*, 4

restructure and have authority over the Orient designed, that is to say, to promote European imperialism and colonialism."[25]

Gramsci's concept of cultural hegemony describes how the ruling class's worldview imposes cultural norms. The doctrine of individualism is not restricted to the West, but contemporary industrial culture approves conscience and rejects interventions of the state. The concept of the Orient is defined in the state and not in society. The notion of "civil society" in Said's *Orientalism*, is a prominent theme in Western philosophy based on the freedom of the individual. Said wrote that culture is operating "within civil society," where impress is not happening through "domination" but "by what Gramsci calls consent"[26]. Said remarked that certain cultural forms and ideas influentially predominate over others, and this "cultural leadership" is what Gramsci has identified as hegemony, or "an indispensable concept for any understanding of cultural life in the industrial West"[27]. Said's broad historical definition of *Orientalism* consists of biographical details of some Western imperialists and lacks historical precision. Although the global centres of capitalism had been established, Said's *Orientalism* continuously persists in the unknown capitalist development and insists on moral or racial superiority of that capitalistic centre. Said revealed that the Oriental always was weaker than the Western. He said Western scholars were aware of contemporary Orientals or Oriental movements of thought and culture, as against "the Orient is all absence, whereas one feels the Orientalist and what he says as presence"[28]. He declared that "the Orient's effective absence [...] clearly places on the Orientalist himself a certain pressure to reduce the Orient in his work, even after he has devoted a good deal of time to elucidating and exposing it"[29] .

Halide Edib Adıvar admits that anyone who is in love with the Eastern mind, approves the spiritual values for the man of the East, but lack of proportion between the spiritual and the material aspects is the problem of Easterns. Edib explains how the East had taken a deeper root in the minds of Turks than the West and also impressed itself on Turk's literature and their personal life. In Pamuk's *Silent House*, a character thinks Easterners "didn't place any importance on" ordinary matters because "nobody in the East is aware of" them, Easterners have been "oppressed for hundreds, thousands of years"[30].

---

[25] *Ibid.*
[26] Said 2003a, 7
[27] *Ibid.*
[28] *Ibid.*, 208
[29] *Ibid.*, 208-9
[30] Pamuk 2012b, 295

He thinks "simple little truth" separates Easterners from Westerners: Westerners have "discovered the bottomless pit of Nothingness," while Easterners "remain unaware of this terrible truth"[31]. He asks, regarding Easterners: "How could it be that for a thousand years not a single person in the East has thought of it. If you think of all the time and the lives that have been lost under this misconception [...] you can see [...] the dimensions of what it has cost"[32] to Easterners. In *The White Castle*, Hoja says, "You're frightened because you believe in me more than I believe in you"[33]. Erdag Göknar says, "The Ottoman past was Orientalized as the Other of republican modernity. Though ostensibly the republican project was to de-Orientalize and de-Ottomanize, the secular modernity espoused by Republican elites actually involved new Orientalizing practices, which targeted appearance, religion, language, and culture as the object of revolutionary transformation"[34]. Orhan Pamuk in *Other Colours* writes everybody can be a Westerner and or an Easterner or a mix of two. He underlined Edward Said's idea of Orientalism but emphasised that because Turkey was never a colony, Turks did not feel the need to romanticise affairs of Turkishness. He explains that Westerners did not humiliate or look down on Turks as any Asian or Middle-Eastern, but only the loss of the Ottoman Empire affected the spirit of the Turkish nation. Pamuk says after the founding of the Republic, Turks desired to Westernize because they were never suppressed by Western powers "but couldn't go far enough"[35]. Turks are suffered from self-infliction because they erased their history "because it was practical"[36]. Pamuk is protesting "self-imposed Westernization" called forth isolation for Turks[37].

---

[31] *Ibid.*, 299
[32] *Ibid.*
[33] Pamuk 2009, 63
[34] Halman 2010, 128
[35] Pamuk 2007, 370-71
[36] *Ibid.* 371
[37] *Ibid.*

Chapter 5

Easternization of the Postmodern Age

Campbell reminds us that there are some obscure matters when we say that the West is "undergoing a process of Easternization"[1]. He asserts some objections against the Easternization thesis. He says the expansion of Eastern values in the West after World War II changed in a way that is not recognizable anymore. Differences that occurred in Western civilization are many because of postmodernization. Campbell reminds us that Christianity did not lose its power and supporters; the individualistic values of the Western worldview are more powerful than they were previously. Huntington observes that both Westerners and non-Westerners point to individualism as "the central distinguishing mark of the West"[2]. Also, Japan and India had "class systems paralleling that of the West"[3].

The most crucial subject in defining the process of Easternization is the impact and interference of postmodernism. Campbell thinks whatever seen as evidence of a decline of the West reflect the decline of modernity[4]. He reminds us that the onset of Easternization in the 1960s coincides with the historical period of separation of the modern from the postmodern. Campbell clarifies differences between postmodern views and the Easternization thesis. He finds that contemporary, Easternized society is more subsequent to Western society than to postmodern society. For him, cultural characteristics that accept the rational structure of the cosmos is more Western than modern society's view. He thinks the new society is post-Western rather than postmodern. Despite talk about the collapse of faith, the postmodernist thesis links to society after modernity, while Easternization captures a wide range of post-Christianity. Campbell affirms that postmodern theorists cannot clarify the mechanism of transformation of modern culture to postmodern society. Despite attempts to affirm cultural changes as a result of a capitalistic worldview of consumerism in postindustrial societies, the Easternization thesis argues that a post-Western culture is the result of a cultural process[5].

---

[1] Campbell 2008, 340
[2] Huntington 1996, 72
[3] *Ibid.*
[4] Campbell 2008, 360
[5] *Ibid.*, 361

Campbell argues that a critical role of rationalization and intellectual development in Western cultural traditions is explicitly mentioned by the Easternization thesis, which clearly reflects the decline of the old and how postmodernist accounts helped to "precipitate the new," that shows "how the decline of the West actually helped bring about the rise of the East in the West"[6].

Campbell mentions that postmodernism may display what has been lost, but it does not clarify significantly what might have been newly replaced in Western culture. Postmodernist Jean-François Lyotard in his collection of essays, *Post-modernism Explained for Children* claims that the postmodern was characterized precisely by a mistrust of the grand narratives of ideas that had formed modernity. Lyotard thinks postmodernity does not believe in universal and general narrative principals of history. This narrative about a narrative or narratives is called metanarrative. Campbell says postmodernism failed to explain the widespread New Age-style Eastern grand-narratives or master narratives that became established in place of metanarratives that were associated with modernity, such as Marxism, Enlightenment, or Progressivism. The question is if postmodernism is against metanarratives, why does it accept the New Age worldview? Campbell assets this conflict reflects that the Easternization thesis announces a "comprehensive" and "accurate" explanation of the changes have already taken place in recent decades in the West "than does postmodernity"[7].

From a postmodern perspective, all knowledge is a narrative form—Lyotard's grand-narratives concern meta-narrative, which talks about one thing after another. Grand-narrative finds interconnection between related events, social systems that try to make sense of history instead of conceiving isolated events in history. Lyotard says that during the postmodern period, people no longer believed in old fashioned grand narratives because they leave out other narratives that may be our narrative. Critical views against modernization are a process inside modernization. Beside urbanization, capitalism, and modernization, Western culture has an intrinsic dream of returning to nature. Postmodernism criticizes the traditional concept of history. It includes sceptical interpretations of culture and literary criticism. The postmodern study distinguishes that worldviews of Eastern and Western are denied. Frederic Jameson was sceptical of metanarratives and thought that because of postmodernity's partially merging of all discourse into a univalent whole, independence in the cultural sphere is lost. He says, "There no longer does […] seem[s] to be any organic relationship between the

---

[6] *Ibid.*, 360-62
[7] *Ibid.*, 362

American history we learn from schoolbooks and the lived experience of the current multinational, high-rise, [the] stagflated city of the newspapers and of our own everyday life"[8].

We can consider the rise of the novel in Turkish literature as a sign of the postmodern globalization period. Postmodernization is related to an incomprehensible collection of opinions, viewpoints, and discourses. Postmodern literature challenges itself through parody. "Parody is both to enshrine the past and to question it. And this is the postmodern paradox"[9]. Postmodern literature can be in conflict with reality, but they kept traditional literary values such as love and death. Postmodern fiction opens itself up to history, to what Edward Said calls the "world." In postmodern literature, this is the "world" of discourse, texts, and intertexts. Bryan Turner reminds us that contemporary postmodern debate is concerned with difference and otherness, and there is a connection between a postmodern critique of universals and the process of indigenization, and both "have a fascination for the textuality of knowledge; its local, embedded, contextual quality and the problems of universalizing or generalizing about 'religion' or 'human nature.'"[10]. Turner explains how postmodernity as a social movement or condition within late capitalism is indirectly related to relativism, irony and parody.[11] He believes differentiation and heterogeneity as a result of cultural diversity help social actors to have a self-reflexive awareness of "the diversity" and problems of their "systems of belief."[12] He says, "Tourism, cultural variation, multiculturalism and the erosion of the sovereignty of the nation-state"end to a self-awareness of the own belief system; so that, postmodernism as "a cultural movement" and postmodernity as "an empirical condition of social systems" are interrelated.[13]

In a general definition, the West or the Western World refers to the continents of Europe, North America, and Australia. In contrast, the East, used by Europeans, refers to Asian societies. It is referred to by Europeans as the Orient, because of mankind's and most Christian churches' original home. Historically, they usually are used as rivals from opposite directions. Huntington says "The West was the West long before it was modern"[14]. He thinks the prominent characteristics of the West "distinguish it from other

---

[8] Jameson 1991, 22
[9] O'Donnell 1989, 6
[10] Turner 1994, 9
[11] *Ibid.*, 17
[12] *Ibid.*
[13] *Ibid.*
[14] Huntington 1996, 69

civilizations" and are more important than "the modernization of the West"[15]. This is the matter we learn from Kaplinsky and Posthuma's *Easternization*, which describes non-Western but modern Japan as an instance to show the difference between modernization and Westernization.

By use of "logocentrism," Derrida asserted that Western culture is based on absolute truths in the thought and behaviour of people. He said Westerners could not get rid of this worldview. Derrida talked about Western civilization and its relation to the non-West or non-Western cultures in a global world. He questioned capitals of cultural hegemony and centralizing authority and said that European cultural identity should not be dispersed into "a myriad of provinces" that are not able to communicate with others or do not translate because of nationalism or jealousy. He says European cultural identity must not accept authority "by means of trans-European cultural mechanisms, by means of publishing, journalistic, and academic concentrations [that] control and standardize, subjecting artistic discourses" in other parts of the world[16]. Charles Bernheimer criticized the Eurocentric study of "non-Western, non-European languages" because "Eurocentric multilingual comparatists have always had their counterparts in the great Orientalists, Sinologists, Indologists" and emphasizes that "being multilingual does not necessarily free one from bigotry"[17]. Indeed, Spengler rejected the Euro-centric view of history. *The Decline of the West* was written before the end of the First World War and demonstrates an approaching tragedy for Europe. He came up with one of the views toward the West to criticize dogmatic Western worldviews. Spengler wrote World-history is the world picture of men of the Western Culture and not all mankind's. He says, "Indian and Classical man formed no image of a world in progress, and perhaps when in due course the civilization of the West is extinguished, there will never again be a Culture and a human type in which "world-history" is so potent a form of the waking consciousness."[18]

Czesław Miłosz thinks Eastern and Western ways of life are different and condemns the specimen Eastern intellectual because he "stumbles upon treacherous appearances, for he finds both imitation and innovation, decadence and vigour, advertised mediocrity and imperfectly recognized greatness"[19]. He criticizes any Eastern intellectual because still, these aspects attract his attention. He thinks the West is a good instance for different mental

---

[15] *Ibid.*
[16] Derrida 1992, 39
[17] Bernheimer 1995, 111
[18] Spengler 1927, 15
[19] Miłosz 1953, 36

creations and "the intellectual understands, of course, that he himself is cosmopolitan since he looks to the West for something"[20]. Czesław Miłosz asserted that Easterners could not take Westerners seriously because they do not comprehend the relativity of thinking habits. He thinks because Easterners have lived in "social order and in a given system of values," they find any other order "unnatural," and it has continued because Easterners found other types "incompatible with human nature"[21]. Miłosz thinks historical hardships taught Easterners to "think sociologically and historically. But it has not freed him from irrational feelings"[22]. Bordieu thinks the Eastern concepts and practices just made a "refract" in "the modern Western habitus back on to itself"[23]. Thus, "Eastern discourse and practice, then, have not simply been appropriated and subsumed by the Western habitus but have actually wrought change by virtue of their ingression into the Western worldview"[24]. He thinks the Easternization thesis is "the fundamental contention that what we have is more of a Westernization of Eastern themes than an Easternization of the Western paradigm," and theosophy and the new age movements are "'counter' to the Western culture"[25].

Bryan Turner thinks that Orientalists "establish their dichotomous ideal type of Western society whose inner essence unfolds in dynamic progress towards democratic industrialism, and Islamic society which is either timelessly stagnant or declines from its inception"[26]. He thinks Middle Eastern societies are defined by the absence of rules, which helps Orientalists "to explain why Islamic civilization failed to produce capitalism, to generate modern personalities, or to convert itself into a secular, radical culture"[27]. By contrast, Edward Said thought the greatest change in Middle East Studies took place because of "cultural opposition to Western domination"[28]. Seyyed Hossein Nasr criticizes wrong interpretations of Easterners' inspiration of Westerners and rigid views toward Eastern Islamic culture because Goethe, for instance, praised Islam and Persian mystic Sufi literature or because Islam contributed to Western science. He says these interpretations are "mostly as a

---

[20] *Ibid.*, 45
[21] *Ibid.*, 28
[22] *Ibid.*
[23] Dawson 2006, 10
[24] *Ibid.*
[25] *Ibid.*
[26] Macfie 2000, 118
[27] *Ibid.*
[28] Said 1983, 315

result of a long period of Western education"²⁹. Halide Edip says, "The religion of the West came to it from the East"³⁰. Moreover, she states that Western philosophy and science have roots from ancient Greece and concepts of civilization from Rome. She continues that although "the West built" on the European continent for the first time, the Romans only synthesized "existing ideas and make a brand new civilisation"³¹.

---

[29] Nasr 2010, 226
[30] Edib 1935, 5
[31] *Ibid.*

Chapter 6

East and West in the Age of Easternization

The relationship between East and West is not a confrontation but a two-way cultural trade of being affected by and influenced by two cultures. Easternization believes that from now on Eastern and Western cultures meet one another as equal partners. Years ago, Halide Edib believed we should use the term "nationhood" instead of "nationalism" because nationalism may cause inner disintegration and conflict. She predicted that the only nations that will be successful in the future would be those that blend materialism and spirituality equally[1]. She wrote, at the time, "the West seems triumphant on the surface. But the East is still there all the same in the soul of the Turk as an undercurrent, and its force is undeniable. When this Eastern element in the Turkish soul develops freely, the future blend of East and West in the Near East might present a model solution for turning what has so far been a conflict into co-operation."[2]

Anthony Appiah uses the word "conversation" for living in peace, which he thinks guarantees agreement about what we think and feel. He thinks conversations bring about imaginative agreement to live together in peace across boundaries of identity by using the ideas and experiences of others: "Conversations does not have to lead to consensus about anything, especially not values; it's enough that it helps people get used to one another"[3]. In defining cross-cultural analysis, Appiah insists on a human sense of communication. After all, he says, we learnt from anthropology that if two social humans share something about real life, common or not, "you can make sense of each other in the end"[4]. Appiah criticizes views that think "personal autonomy is a (usually 'Western') parochialism while group autonomy (often as a 'non-Western' demand) is sacrosanct"[5] and supports liberal multiculturalism, or soft pluralism, considered unbiased neutrality, "as equal respect"[6]. Two people or two societies have lots of things in common for

---

[1] Edib 1935, 222
[2] *Ibid.*, 202
[3] Appiah 2006, 85
[4] *Ibid.*, 99
[5] Appiah 2007, 75
[6] *Ibid.*, 91

dialogue by showing respect for each other's moral values: "The roots of the cosmopolitanism I am defending are liberal: and they are responsive to liberalism's insistence on human dignity"[7]. Appiah defines Richard Rorty's view of accepting universal facts. Rorty rejected that knowledge is able to find correct answers in the world, and the world is independent of Plato's perspectives of truth and goodness. As a result, moral realism or fact-values do not play a key role in defining the relationship between the West and non-West. Appiah says, as Rorty's "ethnocentrism" suggests, "debates within the West are different from debates across a Western/non-Western divide"[8]. In Rorty's view, "something called 'Western culture,' historically contingent as it may be, is what we all share; it is the sea we navigate together, the air we all breathe"[9]. He says Cosmopolitanism imagines a world in which "people are different and welcome to their difference", and it works because there are "common conversations about these shared ideas and objects."[10]

The point is that despite the terms East and West invented by scholars to analyze civilizations, "Westerner" is a unique term that refers to cultures that prefer to label themselves as such. By contrast, the term "Easterner" is rarely used by people living in non-Western countries and is not regularly used by these countries' members. And the term "Easterner" and "Westerner" are nothing without the other. Homi Bhabha reminds "human identity as an image […] are inscribed in the sign of resemblance"[11]. He says that Third World voices "speak within and to discourses familiar to the 'West'"[12]. He thinks that "The Third World, far from being confined to its assigned space, has penetrated the inner sanctum of the 'First World' in the process of being 'Third Worlded'—arousing, inciting, and affiliating with the subordinated others in the First World" with hopes to "connect with minority voices"[13]. He asserts that Third World voices should not change the narratives of their histories, but transform their "sense of what it means to live," in another time and place.[14]

Eastern themes have been popular in the West because they have offered novelty to the modern Western aesthetic. Eastern concepts and practices in the West changed in a way that new paradigms are "more of a Westernization

---

[7] *Ibid.*, 267
[8] *Ibid.*, 253
[9] *Ibid.*, 253-54
[10] *Ibid.*, 258
[11] Bhabha 1994, 70
[12] *Ibid.*, 354
[13] *Ibid.*
[14] *Ibid.*, 367

of Eastern themes than an Easternization of the Western paradigm"[15]. Dawson warns that the "Easternization thesis itself, in framing its analysis as an 'East meets West' scenario, toys dangerously with this risk in so far as it talks of East and West as if they were undifferentiated cultural entities rather than the mosaic heterogeneities we know them to be"[16]. Dawson says that nowadays, Easterner "concepts and practices are uncoupled from their cultural and performative contexts, denuded of their original meaning, and rendered palatable to the established predilections of the Western aesthetic" in a transposition process of "the cosmological worldview"[17] or new cosmos self-realization. A woman in Pamuk's *My Name is Red* murmurs these woes: "My fickle heart longs for the West when I'm in the East and for the East when I'm in the West." [18] She amuses herself "frontside and backside," to be "Eastern and Western both"[19]. In a discussion about East and West in *My Name is Red*, when Stork suggests that Butterfly should "head" West instead of East, Butterfly answers, "God belongs to the East and the West"[20] and continues an artist should not "succumb to hubris of any kind", and apart from the matter of East or West, he should paint the way he sees.

During the 1960s in Iran, Jalal Al-Ahmed published a book under the title *Occidentosis: A Plague from the West* and its title was used as a term to mean *Westoccification* or *West-struck-ness*. The book described the loss of Iranian cultural identity because of the adoption and imitation of Western cultural models. He simulated Westernization and Western materialism to cholera or sawflies in the wheat fields. He argued that Iran becomes a producer rather than a consumer. For him, the poles of East and West were defined based on industrialization or consumerism. Later, an Iranian revolutionary sociologist, Ali Shariati combined traditional Islamic themes with modern cultural points of view such as Marxism. His books had a significant effect on the Iranian Islamic Revolution of 1979. As a matter of fact, one can confront Eastern characteristics in a Western-style civilization and conversely. If we accept that the origin of Western culture was Ancient Hellenistic Greek, there was a fierce competition with another exemplary civilization of the Orient, Persia. Persian civilization was not a place inhabited by barbarians, but a land of the arts, architecture, and fashions. Campbell thinks that the idea of "the West"

---

[15] Dawson 2006, 3
[16] *Ibid.*
[17] Dawson 2006, 8
[18] Pamuk 2001, 431
[19] *Ibid.*
[20] *Ibid.*, 488

created by the ancient Greeks against the alien threat from the East (Persia), which it afterwards overcame, allowed the Greeks to develop the continuing idea of superior Western civilization against defeated Eastern civilization. Islam at one time represented the greatest military power on earth. The Ottoman Empire invaded Europe, Africa, China, and India. The greatest economic power in the world lost its position due to scientific and technological progress in Europe after the Renaissance. Then patriotism and nationalism entered into the Ottoman political directory. The first was from Western Europe, and the latter was from central and Eastern Europe, and they brought new definitions of identity to the Middle Eastern Ottoman community. For Edward Said, there was a "contrast between White Occidentalism and colored Orientalism"[21]. Non-Western scholars want to have their own Occidentalism. Scholars in non-Western societies do not like to share common Western academic Occidentalisms because those Occidentalisms have shaped Western interpretations of non-Western societies.

Occidentalism represents images of the West which is the counterpart to the term Orientalism and identifies representations of Westerners based on evidence in works of Chinese, Japanese, and Indian art from old times up until now. Occidentalism studies how the Eastern-world stands against the socio-economic forces of modernization that originated in Western culture and revealed the influence of Western ideas upon Eastern intellectuals. James Carrier defines Occidentalism as "the growing concern with kastom (in Melanesia), the 'invention of tradition,' the creation of distinctive identities by people outside the West"[22]. Couze Venn defines it as the "conceptual and historical space in which a particular narrative of the subject and a particular narrative of history have been constituted; these have become hegemonic with modernization, having effects throughout the world because of the universal scope of the project of modernity and the global reach of European colonization"[23]. According to Venn, Occidentalism means "the process of the becoming West of Europe and the becoming modern of the world" in "the space of intelligibility of a triumphalist modernity and to the genealogy of the present as a history of the transformations that have in the course of time instituted the forms of sociality and the lifeworlds"[24]. Western captives or traders in the East who escaped and returned home wrote of their adventures in the mysterious Orient, but Eastern captives or rare traders in the West did not write their experiences in literary

---

[21] Said 2003, 253
[22] Carrier 2003, viii-ix
[23] Venn 2000, 2
[24] *Ibid.*, 8

works. Thus, the Occident remained more mysterious than the Orient. For years, there were no Occidentalists in the Orient.

For the whole of the nineteenth and most of the twentieth century, the search for wealth and power were the main aspects of the West. Bernard Lewis thinks Islam was the first eager religion to make progress toward a universal mission, but today, modern Western civilization is the dominant civilization in defining modernity. But I think that despite cultural change into Westernization in Eastern countries, Westernization was not an essential part of modernization, even if it were possible to modernize without Westernizing the culture. Westerners are more aware of the diversity and complexity of Islamic traditions nowadays. As Turner reminds us, Orientalism explains the "progressive features of the Occident" and "the social stationariness of the Orient"[25]. Edward Said tells us that Western-style universalism derives from European Enlightenment thought, and even globalism cannot overcome the cultural divisions that Western-style hegemonic universalism causes. In many Third World societies, this conflict results in intense questioning of self-identity and identity crisis. Global Westernization is not possible without restrictions in geographically confined cultural contexts. Orientalism, as Said says, is "all of which together formed a simulacrum of the Orient and reproduced it materially in the West, for the West"[26].

To become an other or to assume someone else's position makes a fantastic world, as shown in Pamuk's works. Being the other or imagining an other, is the central theme of his novels. After the Tanzimat period in Turkey, the cultural desire to follow Westerners in Turkey in the process of Westernization is obvious. The Kemalist government was deeply influenced by Western ideas and made reform and created a new secular legal system based on the model of Westernization. The grandfather of *Silent House* says, "I accept that the Europeans found everything before we did and investigated it all down to the smallest detail"[27]. He hopes to "establish a brand-new world" with fresh thoughts in Turkey, which is "a world of freedom such as the East has never seen, a paradise of logic on the face of the earth," in a way "better than the West" because they will find their mistakes and they "won't repeat them"[28]. He hopes to raise his children as "free and independent person[s]" who will not learn "the Eastern melancholy, the weeping, pessimism, the defeat of our

---

[25] Turner 1994, 22
[26] Said 2003a, 166
[27] Pamuk 2012b, 147
[28] *Ibid.*, 97

terrible Oriental fatalism"[29], and this is the only way for Turks who hope to go back to their delightful history. In *The White Castle*, the Italian tries to convince Hoja about his "superiority" and "independence"[30]. In another part, Hoja accepts the Occidental mind, and the Italian, who now represents the oriental mind, criticizes the Occidental view of Hoja by saying, "He'd written that we were now in decline, described our minds as if they were dirty cupboards filled with old junk. He'd said we could not be reformed, that if we were to survive our only alternative was to submit immediately, and after this, we would not be able to do anything for centuries but imitate those to whom we had surrendered"[31]. The novel shows another view of the Occidental mind through an Oriental point of view: "He said he'd come to know and love me; he expressed his astonishment: how two people who'd lived together so many years could resemble each other so little, how they could be so unlike one another, he could not understand"[32]. In *The New Life*, "the book" can be identified as the Occidental mind that affects the Oriental mind. Giving chapter and verse to modernization, the protagonist, Galip, confronts a question in a book that wonders, why after two hundred years we still not "caught up with the West?"[33].

Moreover, identity plays a crucial role in the struggle of East and West. Huntington defined identity as an individual or a group's self-consciousness to distinguish themselves from others. As grown-up human comprehends his hypothetical identities by name or citizenship after being grown up—the elements he owned but could not comprehend before—identity is perceptible through relations with others. It means that individuals define their identity through a group or through many groups. The latter identity is incommutable. Huntington adds, "so long as people interact with others, they have no choice, but to define themselves in relation to those others and identify their similarities with and differences from those others"[34]. He approves Benedict Anderson's theory and asserts that as people define their identities under pressure or freely as they wish, free choice cannot put itself into effect. Although "identities are imagined selves: they are what we think we are and what we want to be," but they may be redefined or rejected and change over

---

[29] *Ibid.*
[30] Pamuk 2009, 60
[31] *Ibid.*, 143
[32] *Ibid.*, 144
[33] Pamuk 2006a, 303
[34] Huntington 2004, 22

time as happened to the term "race"[35]. In addition, multiple identities depend on national, cultural, political, and social elements, which change over time. Multiple identities may even conflict with each other. Huntington emphasizes that identities are based on interactions with others. Although they are self-termed and individual, they are redefined in new social situations. Thus, government and environment assign identities to people. Situations and interactions define an individual's identity, and people's observation of identity distinguish them from others.

Benedict Anderson symbolizes human consciousness. He draws an analogy by picturing an adult who does not remember childhood, so that early consciousness is a vanished memory. He compares remaining photographs to scrawled yellowed pictures. Recorded diaries, letters, and photos of a person in his teens are linked to the present: now grown up, the person wants to know about his past, but because it is forgotten, it must be narrated. Being more grown up helps the person to find his real identity. The conflict of defining identity is exemplified by Huntington. He thinks that a sense of national identity is a strategy to differentiate one person from other people with a different language, history, or religion. Huntington defines culture as "people's language, religious beliefs, social and political values, assumptions as to what is right and wrong, appropriate and inappropriate, and to the objective institutions and behavioral patterns that reflect these subjective elements"[36].

Anthony Appiah says that beginning in infancy, we are in dialogue with other people to comprehend who we are and to develop a conception of our identity, articulated through concepts and practices in school, religion, and also interactions from our earliest years with others. As Aristotle stated, we are social beings. Appiah thinks collective identities are the collective aspects of our individual identities, which respond to social conceptions about how a person of a distinct identity behaves. He says personal histories and narratives of the individual self, like novels, are essential in the structure of collective identities. Furthermore, national and ethnic identities fit a personal narrative into a larger narrative. Because different people have different identities, universal values of solidarity are different too. Isaiah Berlin's sceptical term, Positive Liberty, which is about freedom from internal constraints, is used by Appiah to remind us that governments shape people in the name of better selves through the construction of new identities. Identification is the transformation of a subject by the model the other

---

[35] *Ibid.*
[36] *Ibid.*, 30

provides, used to verify aspects of a person's identity in the process of the construction of one's identity through reference to available identities.

Identity is a reaction to create a focus. It means that, through describing that you are not part of "them," you can show that you are part of "us." So we get our identity in a time process, after birth. Pamuk says, "We are troubled by the abundance of rumours about where we come from, who we are, where we're going, and who drew us"[37]. In *The White Castle*, the main characters try to answer the question, "Why am I what I am?" The Venetian says, "this question is often asked by them"[38]. Hoja, as an Easterner, asked this question "without knowing they did"[39], and Westerners asked it before. The Venetian thought he is not able to help Hoja to answer this question because "this was something he had to do for himself"[40]. To make Hoja aware of his identity, he gives Hoja his "last book about gazelles and sparrows being content because they never reflected on themselves and knew nothing of what they were"[41].

---

[37] Pamuk 2007, 326
[38] Pamuk 2009, 48
[39] *Ibid.*, 49
[40] *Ibid.*
[41] *Ibid.*, 133

Chapter 7

Easternization is the Other of Itself

Immanuel Kant believed it is not possible to reach an understanding through experience restricted in time and place. Under the effect of Kant, Hegel asserted that the world is meaningful and the first step in philosophical research is the courage to see the truth. Through the Hegelian dialectical vantage point, which posits the out rational control of the world, the West created the idea of gaining freedom from the rest of the world. Later, by acknowledging otherness, it chose the process of assimilation, incorporation, and self-congratulation. Derrida defines "supplementation," which is the relationship between two hierarchies, and Western culture is based on that. Western culture finds light better than darkness. Derrida uses Supplementation to define the relationship between two different hierarchies to prove that they support and need each other. Another post-structuralist, Roland Barthes, uses another term similar to Derrida's 'binary opposition," called "symbolic code," about the pairing of binary polarities like male/female and day/night. The ambivalent unconscious use of otherness makes it more complicated. If we consider those as "others", who are different from "us," the difference of those different "others" is the same. I do not find it an unconscious view, but a nonconscious view because of lacking any element of consciousness in the context. Turner explained to find a resolution to the problems of the Orientalist tradition, "a genuinely global perspective"[1] is required. He thinks anthropology should be "directed towards the otherness of Western culture in order to dislodge the privileged position of dominant Western cultures"[2]. Derrida explains Western high-handedness in defining otherization by telling "what is proper to a culture is to not be identical to itself. Not to not have an identity, but not to be able to identify itself, to be able to say 'me' or 'we'; to be able to take the form of a subject only in the non-identity to itself."[3] He says there is no self-relation, or relation to oneself, and no identification with oneself without culture, but "a culture of oneself is a culture of the other, a

---

[1] Turner 1994, 104
[2] *Ibid.*, 104
[3] Derrida 1992, 9

culture of the double genitive and of the difference to oneself. The grammar of the double genitive also signals that a culture never has a single origin."[4]

In Pamuk's *The White Castle*, Hoja and the Venetian sit "at the two ends of the table"[5] and try to answer a question, "why we were what we were"[6]. In a twilight room that symbolizes the Republic of Turkey, they sit on two sides of a table, the darker part of which represents the East, and the brighter side represents the West. They try to answer a question that reveals their identity and cultural background. It shows that humankind's search to find a pure and unadulterated identity is nonsense because everybody experiences the same world despite the fact that they do not experience it as the same. The Ottoman army has to capture Doppio Castle to proclaim victory. Doppio in Italian means "double" and "two-faced." It is the last gate of the conquest of the East against the West, which can't be "captured despite all efforts"[7]. Doppio is an ideal aim that is never captured completely. Although Pamuk consciously represents what we called Easternization, unconsciously he is not completely sure about the process of Easternization. The Venetian and the Hoja, through arguments about their past, find that "the truth of their identity is found in the cathartic purging of the memory through the admittance of former wrong doings"[8]. The stories of the past that they write and exchange are a "distorting mirror for the selves" that helps in "self-conception"[9] of one's self and other's identities. Afridi explains, "The slave becomes a point of fixation for the Hoja upon which he projects alternately the desire to be like him as a model of power and knowledge, and conversely as the other against which he can define himself as different and unique"[10]. *The White Castle* is full of parts in which "He" and "the Other" change places or are treated as one: "'Now I am like you,' he said. 'I know your fear. I have become you!'[...] He claimed he could see the world as I did; 'they,' he was saying again, now at last he understood how 'they' thought, how 'they' felt"[11]; or, "While I looked apprehensively into his face, I felt an impulse to say 'I am I.' It was as if, had I been able to find the courage to speak this nonsensical phrase"[12]; or, "Was it

---

[4] *Ibid.*, 10
[5] Pamuk 2009, 63
[6] *Ibid.*
[7] *Ibid.*, 125
[8] Afridi 2012, 69
[9] *Ibid.*
[10] Afridi 2012, 70
[11] Pamuk 2009, 72
[12] *Ibid.*, 109

not the best proof that men everywhere were identical with one another that they could take each other's place?"[13].

Pamuk criticizes Western Orientalists because they define Eastern believers as "a pantheist or as a thinker influenced by Plotinus, Pythagoras, and the Kabbalah," but do not accept them as a "pure man of the East"[14]. The loss of the idea of mystery turns the East into "the slave of the West"[15]. At the end of *The Black Book*, Galip started to write in Celâl's newspaper column, that he gazed into the mirror, "read" his face and dreamed of becoming the person he "longed to become"[16]. He says they have learned to live together over the years[17]. In postmodernism, the "different" comes to be defined in particularizing terms as ethnicity, race, and national orientation, while the Other is widely used to denote not the same. Michel De Certeau wrote that "Western thought has always thematized the other as a threat to be reduced, as a potential same-to-be, a yet-not-same"[18].

Arasteh describes a Sufi's journey as a cosmic creature through unconscious consciousness. Not finding real self in religion or other sources, Rumi, at last, finds it potentially within himself and actually within Shams and the universal self-observed through Shams state of being. Rumi loved the new image when he was close to becoming one with Shams' image that no one could differentiate them from the other. He saw that Shams' image and Shams' soul was so close to his own that even he knew whatever Shams might think, and said, "In every breath the color of my heart takes the color of his thought"[19]. This is the route men took in the process of making "he-ness" into "I-ness." Although he is the same, he can gain a better union with all by allowing himself to be reborn. Arasteh describes Rumi confronted with two kinds of conflicts: "Inwardly, he experienced a conflict between what he was and what he envisioned he would become, that is, between the limited 'self' given by his training in culture, and that self which would be the outcome of his relatedness to the universe, to the whole of humanity"[20]. The outward conflict appeared between "his new orientation and that which the public demanded, that is, between his new path toward change and that of

---

[13] *Ibid.*, 136
[14] Pamuk 2006a, 303
[15] *Ibid.*, 320
[16] *Ibid.*, 326
[17] *Ibid.*, 40
[18] De Certeau 2000, xiii
[19] Arasteh 1974, 70
[20] *Ibid.*, 46

traditional ways. In other words, the removal required a transmutation, which, in turn, depended upon tearing aside the veil and overcoming mental blocks"[21]. Rumi notices that men should eliminate the "I" in order to become "not-I" in the unitary world. He preferred "the experience of becoming a universal self instead of being a prominent Muslim theologian"[22] . Arasteh explains Rumi's self-awareness that his real self in contrast to the phenomenal self, is "the cosmic self or universal self"[23] and the product of culture. Unconsciously, phenomenal self encompasses consciousness and "possesses infinite potentialities while consciousness is limited" and "only the unconscious provides the means of attaining the real self."[24] He says, "The cosmic self embraces all our being while the phenomenal self constitutes only a part of our existence. The phenomenal self has separated us from our origin, that of union with all of life."[25] Being aware of this separation, "we can only live fully by emptying consciousness, bringing to light the unconscious achieving insight into our whole existence, and living in a state of complete awareness."[26] Arasteh calls this state "cosmic existence or transcendental consciousness" in which the real self can be thought of as "the crown of the unconscious, which is potentially conscious existence, the Sufi's goal."[27]

Homi Bhabha, by quoting from Lacan, refers to the Lacanian vision of subjectivity, mimicry acts as camouflage and uses in describing the cultural politics of colonialism. Lacan studies orders of otherness in relation to the subject. According to him, one of the most significant conditions of possibility for singular subjectivity is the collective symbolic order or "the big Other"[28]. Lacan capitalizes the Other and emphasizes an innovative theory of the subject. For Lacan, the symbolic "I" is distinct from the imaginary "ego": "I is an other"[29]. He says "the subject is decentered in relation to the individual"[30]. Lacan's notion of subjectivity is modelled by the mirror stage and the practice of mimicry. In his famous work *The Wretched of the Earth*, Frantz Fanon concerns himself with the production of subjectivity, which "is no longer taken as the starting point for modifying the individual's attitude. On the

---

[21] *ibid.*
[22] *Ibid.*, 45
[23] *Ibid.*, 42
[24] *Ibid.*
[25] *Ibid.*
[26] *Ibid.*, 43
[27] *Ibid.*
[28] Lacan 1991, 235
[29] *Ibid.*, 7
[30] *Ibid.*, 9

contrary, the emphasis is on the body, which is broken in the hope that the national consciousness will disintegrate. The individual is knocked into shape"[31]. Homi Bhaba examines the relationship between Fanon's analysis of European man and his colonized other, and Lacan's reading of subjectivity is characterized by an idealized mental image of the oppressed unconscious one.

Exploring problems of subjectivity and authenticity among cultures is the backbone of Said's *Orientalism*. Through deconstructionism, Said was able to analyse historically and socially what people understand by the notion of Otherness and Other. His critique arrays images of other people, thereby enabling us to conceive the relationship between ourselves and the Other in different terms. Said insists that Western perception of the Orient is false and without reference to what the Orient actually is. Alexander Macfie says, "While we need to be aware also of the danger of turning the 'Other' into an ill-defined universal, we need at the same time to be conscious of the contrary danger of relativizing the 'Other' to the extent that the context of the ethnographic encounter in time and space is lost, and both observer and observed are reduced to a common denominator in which it becomes increasingly difficult to extricate one from the other"[32]. Richard Fox says anthropology's aim is the "study of man," which historically is divided between the West and the rest. "It has been and continues to be primarily the study of the non-Western other by the Western self, even if in its new guise it seeks explicitly to give voice to the Other or to present a dialogue between the self and other, either textually or through an explication of the fieldwork encounter"[33]. The Eurocentric world view of the past by its Orientalistic corollaries of colonialism is preoccupied with "otherness". Appiah is sampling the Argument of "Other Cultures" which manifest itself in terms of "Us and Them," "the West and the Rest," "atomistic" and "holistic" conceptions of society, or "liberals and communitarians" in the context of "astronomer who mistakes the fly on the other end of the telescope for a planet a good deal farther away."[34] MacKenzie is elucidating that always there was "a defensive perimeter called "the West" around anything done by individual nations or persons who constituted a self-appointed Western essence in themselves" that guards change[35]. This tactic was "supposed contamination brought forward threateningly by the very existence of the Other" and "permits

---

[31] Fanon 2004, 215-16
[32] Macfie 2000, 215
[33] Fox 1991, 139
[34] Appiah 2007, 45
[35] MacKenzie 1995, 215

a comforting retreat into an essentialised, basically unchanging Self"; eventually, there is a move "to freeze the Other in a kind of basic objecthood."[36]

Dialectical method is a discourse holding different views that have been central to European and Indian philosophy since antiquity. Through dialectics, Pamuk brings about an anti-Hegelian rational dialectic world targeting otherness. Bhabha wrote "Other" represents "a culturally alien consciousness" and "negation of a primordial identity—cultural or psychic— that introduces the system of differentiation which enables the cultural to be signified as a linguistic, symbolic, historic reality."[37] He emphasized that the Other is not an "It-self, a front of identity, truth or misrecognition."[38]

As the hero represents his condition, we find his problems as our own. Thus, in the act of reading others' stories, we identify ourselves with heroes. It is crucial to combine general and individual aspects of "self" and "other" by putting ourselves in the shoes of the protagonist. Hereby "literature presents us with a new 'rational' image of independency. According to this image, while retaining our own particularities, we can remain in close connection with others, not being cut off from them"[39]. In *Silent House*, When a character asks Doctor Selahattin about "they" who he repeatedly is "talking about," he answers that "they" refers back to "the Europeans, the Westerners"[40]. Selahattin resembles "the West and the Renaissance," and "the East and time" to other oppositions such as "science and Allah [...] night and day, fire and water [...] and death and life"[41]. Using "Him" with a capital "H," the narrator when he talks about Hoja in Chapter 11 of *The White Castle*, represents an Occidental view of the Other. "Him" or the Other represents the exchange of power and knowledge between East and West.

Social knowledge and national-discovery play an essential role in contact with otherness in the Western context. In its general definition, the nation is considered as a community of specific cultural values and customs. This cultural community is defined by the history of their descendants. A nation is a population or group that consciously have the same national identity. A consciously increasing sense of national identity based on group values makes nationalist doctrine. Nationalism in an individual and collective sense treats as a historical movement and finds the world as a product of various

---

[36] *Ibid.*
[37] Bhabha 1994, 74
[38] *Ibid.*
[39] Yamanaka 2006, 77
[40] Pamuk 2012b, 100
[41] *Ibid.*, 102

communities with their own history. Group identity is described by a sense of differentiating "us" and "them" under the title "ethnicity." Culture, history, and language similarities of culture make people feel responsible for each other as parts of the same whole called "nation." Pamuk is aware of a reflected shame in his relations with the West. In *Other Colours,* he mentions the tensions between tradition and modernity in Turkey which is the source of East-West challenge and Turkey's relations with Europe. He links the sense of shame of anger, defeat and humiliation with a proud nationalistic pride. He reminds the glory of the Ottoman Empire that was "knocking on Europe's door," but yet "these emotions of fragility can, from time to time, take flame and rage unchecked."[42]

Talât Halman asserts Pamuk's Ottoman theme in literary works is a "meeting place of the real and the imaginary, of self and other, a space of political negotiation, of transgression, and even of the sublime"[43]. Hasan of *Silent house* thinks that "it will be the court of history and the judgment of the nation" that decides whether nations were loyal to "the Turkish traditions that have come down over thousands of years"[44]. In contrast, another character in *Silent house* thinks that America and the Soviets as symbols of the East and the West trying to "divide up the world" through "nationalism"[45]. He thinks they tried to divide Turkey by asking "Are you first a Muslim or a Turk?" because they were aware that "the center of the world was the Middle East and the key to the Middle East was Turkey"[46]. Bernard Lewis's view is entirely different from Pamuk's character in the novel. Lewis wrote when things are going badly, Middle Eastern people are accusing past and present because it is "easier and always more satisfying to blame others for one's misfortunes"[47] For Arabs, nationalism as an imported term from Europe, produced new perceptions through which "Arabs could lay the blame for their troubles on the Turks who had ruled them for many centuries. Turks could blame the stagnation of their civilization on the dead weight of the Arab past in which the creative energies of the Turkish people were caught and immobilized. Persians could blame the loss of their ancient glories on Arabs, Turks, and Mongols impartially." Thus, in the nineteenth and twentieth centuries, the

---

[42] Pamuk 2007, 231
[43] Halman 2010, 135
[44] Pamuk 2012b, 210
[45] *Ibid.,* 1
[46] *Ibid.,* 180-81
[47] Lewis 2002, 169

period of British and French paramountcy in the Middle East "produced a new and more plausible scapegoat—Western imperialism."[48]

Anthony Appiah thinks that "a nation [...] is an 'imagined community' of traditions or ancestry running beyond the scale of the face-to-face and seeking political expression for itself"[49]. He says "historical ascent, nationalism, which is often contrasted with individualism, can equally seem to be a spawn of individualism"[50]. Although Halide Edib reminds us that human anatomy is the same all over the world. She clarifies that historical impacts are not important to define a nation, because the masses are there to produce magnificent monuments for the use and the happiness of the few, and as a result, the contributions of every individual in a nation are not equal. Benedict Anderson in *Imagined Communities* asserts that dynastic, cultural, linguistic, and ideology binds, ties people together in a community: "today, even the most insular nations accept the principle of naturalization, no matter how difficult in practice they may make it"[51]. Naturalization is the past legal process whereby a non-citizen in a country may acquire citizenship or nationality of that country. Homi Bhaba criticized Anderson's view by stating, "Anderson resists a reading of the modern nation that suggests that the hybridity of the colonial space may provide a pertinent problematic within which to write the history of the 'postmodern' national formations of the West"[52]. Edward Said also believed that "All nationalist cultures depend heavily on the concept of national identity"[53].

---

[48] *Ibid.*, 169-70
[49] Appiah 2007, 244
[50] *Ibid.*, 238
[51] Anderson 1991, 145
[52] Bhabha 1994, 359
[53] Said 1983, 267

Chapter 8

Easternization for Pamuk as a Turk

The conflict of defining identity is exemplified by Huntington: "Turks have been conflicted over whether they should think of themselves primarily as European, Western, Muslim, Middle Eastern, or even Central Asian"[1]. Pamuk wonders about identity definitions because "on the one hand Turks have a legitimate need to defend their national dignity, and this includes being recognized as part of the West and Europe"[2], and at the same time there's also the fear of losing identity in the course of Westernization because they find "Westernization as a poor imitation" of a new culture[3]. Pamuk criticizes opponents who "ignite every possible political passion—from nationalism to Islamism"[4] in themselves. He attached credence to his theory that Turkey should not worry about having two spirits, souls or different cultures, because "if you worry too much about one part of you killing the other, you'll be left with a single spirit."[5] He finds this feeling like a "sickness" and asserts "I try to propagate it in Turkish politics, among Turkish politicians who demand that the country should have one consistent soul—that it should belong to either the East or the West or be nationalistic. I'm critical of that monistic outlook."[6]

Pamuk thinks "Mediterranean identity" was defined by "non-Mediterraneans" much better than Mediterraneans themselves[7]. Pamuk thinks if a writer wants to find out Mediterranean identity, "he must give up certain other identities. For example, a French writer who wants to be the Mediterranean must give up a part of his Frenchness. By the same logic, a Greek writer wishing to be the Mediterranean must give up part of his Balkan and European identities."[8] In *Other Colours*, Pamuk says, the sense of belonging to a place is possible through having no knowledge of its boundaries, its image, or its existence; calling deridingly the best İstanbullu is "the one who has forgotten that he is one," or

---

[1] Huntington 2004, 24
[2] Pamuk 2005, 1
[3] *ibid.*
[4] *ibid.*
[5] Pamuk 2007, 369
[6] *ibid.*
[7] *Ibid.*, 196
[8] *Ibid.*, 196

the most authentic Muslim "has no idea of what is Islamic and what is not!"[9] Starting from this point of view, Pamuk says he had "an image of the Mediterranean" but not the Istanbul in which he lived and accepted as "a darker, grayer, and more northern city than the notion of 'Mediterranean' could accommodate"[10]. Pamuk believes the Mediterranean belonged to inferior and different peoples and this illusion and confusion, reflects "Turkey's awkwardness and uncertainty about the Mediterranean."[11] Pamuk says, "I'm not mourning the Ottoman Empire. I'm a Westernizer. I'm pleased that the Westernization process took place. I'm just criticizing the limited way in which the ruling elite—meaning both the bureaucracy and the new rich—had conceived of Westernization."[12] Pamuk lend credence to the idea that lack of necessary confidence in Turks to create a rich national culture in its own rituals is on the score of Turks' inability in strive to "create an Istanbul culture that would be an organic combination of East and West"; and it can be said that they just "put Western and Eastern things together."[13] Notwithstanding a fading local Ottoman culture, Turks need to "invent a strong local culture, which would be a combination—not an imitation—of the Eastern past and the Western present."[14] Pamuk has carried out this ideology into literature and says, "I try to do the same kind of thing in my books. Probably new generations will do it, and entering the European Union will not destroy Turkish identity but make it flourish and give us more freedom and self-confidence to invent a new Turkish culture."[15] He deliberates imitating the West or "old dead Ottoman culture" is not the solution and Turks should not have anxiety about belonging to any of them completely.[16]

Benedict Anderson and Bhabha's definitions of nation and identity separate the national Self from the foreign Other. Thus it is necessary to define these identities through the terms Oriental or Occidental. Pamuk follows the process of Easternization and tries to phase out differences during the detachment process of belonging to Orient or Occident. In the Western worldview, cultural assertions of both the West and the Oriental Other are equally attractive. From the eighteenth century on, after decreasing anxiety against the Turks in central Europe, uncritical eagerness toward everything

---

[9] *Ibid.*, 194
[10] *Ibid.*
[11] *Ibid.*
[12] *Ibid.*, 369
[13] *Ibid.*
[14] *Ibid.*
[15] *Ibid.*
[16] *Ibid.*, 369

Turkish and Oriental increased. Western colonialism never happened in Turkey, but some Turkish nationalists think a kind of inner-colonization or self-colonization happened during the modernization period. Halide Edib says, "The Ottoman Turks are a race as mixed as the Americans. Greeks, Slavs, Italians, Hungarians, Albanians, especially Circassians and people of every possible race in the Near East have been as individuals or as groups assimilated, converted and Turkicised. Therefore, there is very little of the original Turkish race left"[17]. Gokalp thought, "By the term Turkish-Islamic civilization, we mean a 'community' civilization. There can be a 'society' civilization common to all Ottoman 'communities.' This Ottoman civilization will consist of a local manifestation of the universal 'society' civilization"[18]. Edip described Turkey as the best place to research the East and the West's contradiction: "Both the Imperial Turkey of old and present Republican Turkey are placed where the East and West meet geographically, namely, the Near East, an area that has bred typically Eastern and Western nations and civilisations, and has been the contending ground of all philosophical, cultural, political ideas and ideologies and human forces"[19]. She thinks "Turkey is an ideal cross-section of the human world, the very best laboratory in which a student of history can make his researches on the conflict of East and West"[20]. Edip reminds us that the New West had entered the Ottoman world as a method in thought during the reform period, called Tanzimat. Tanzimat blended East and West by interpreting Western ideas and forms "and incorporated [them] in what Turkey had inherited from the old East, without the old or the new upsetting the balance"[21]. Pamuk explains that after writing *The White Castle*, like the Hoja and Venetian characters, the anxiety of being influenced by someone else "resembles Turkey's position when it looks west."[22] He criticizes the spirit of looking European or the sense of becoming Westernized and then "being accused of not being authentic enough," which is similar to "the relationship between competitive brothers."[23] Pamuk finds happiness of his nation without becoming European slave or mocking them. He says, "I refuse to be a European, and I won't ape their ways. I'm going to live out my own history and be no one but myself."[24] Pamuk reminds Europhiles idea

---

[17] Edib 1935, 113
[18] Gokalp 1959, 102
[19] Edib 1935, 1
[20] *ibid.*
[21] *Ibid.*, 54
[22] Pamuk 2007, 368
[23] *Ibid.*
[24] Pamuk 2004, 331

that to be a true Westerner, a person must first become an individual. Pamuk shows his hand by telling that he is "standing up against the Westerners as an individual; it's because I am an individual that I refuse to imitate them."[25]

Pamuk was educated in Western-oriented schools, and his point of view toward Turkish society is considered both Western and Oriental by critics. However, Pamuk's books greatly mirror Turkish culture. Pamuk says, "I don't believe in, say, a clash of civilizations…. I am living in a culture where the clash of East and West, or the harmony of East and West, is the lifestyle. That is Turkey"[26]. Pamuk criticizes Western intellectuals during the past two centuries because they were convinced that Istanbul and Turkey as a whole do not have any connections to the West. But where Turks feel "irritation and scorn, they feel reverence and longing, and this sends them into an identity crisis"[27]. Pamuk says "they are obliged to pass over his disparaging comments in silence; as they stand on the edge of Europe, torn between West and East, they are obliged to put even more faith in Europe than André Gide did"[28]. Istanbul has a cosmopolitan nature with inhabitants from different ethnic and religious backgrounds. According to Azade Seyhan, in a prominent Istanbul author, Ahmet Hamdi Tanpınar's works, Istanbul "embodies both the trauma of separation from a long-standing heritage and the recuperative potential of the residue of that heritage"[29]. Pamuk reminds us of the "powerless historian" of Nietzsche's *Use and Abuse of History* and asserts that *hüzün* is the process of changing the history of an Istanbullu's city to "into the history of himself"[30]. According to Pamuk, "*hüzün*" is an "emotion, which we feel as something between physical pain and grief," that in Turkish literature acts as a "grief that no one can or would wish to escape, an ache that finally saves our souls and also gives them depth"[31]. He perceives the hüzün of Istanbul out of an individual's standing against society, but, "an erosion of the will to stand against the values and mores of the community" and "honoring the virtues of harmony, uniformity, humility."[32] Hüzün teaches "endurance in times of poverty and deprivation", encourages us to "read life and the history of the city" and allows the people of Istanbul not to find Istanbul's history as

---

[25] *Ibid.*
[26] Lavery 2003, 1
[27] Pamuk 2007, 209
[28] *Ibid.*
[29] Seyhan 2008, 136
[30] Pamuk 2006b, 167
[31] *Ibid.*, 104
[32] *Ibid.*

an incurable illness to be endured like grief, "to be viewed and judged in black and white" but a matter of honor.[33]

Hüzün-stricken *Istanbullus* have the same attitude toward Istanbul, and it is "something the entire city feels together and affirms as one"[34]. Alberto Manguel wrote that *hüzün* is a Turkish word with "Arabic root (it appears five times in the Koran) that denotes a feeling of deep spiritual loss but also a hopeful way of looking at life... For the Sufis, *hüzün* is the spiritual anguish one feels at not being close enough to God; for Saint John of the Cross, this anguish causes the sufferer to plummet so far down that his soul will, as a result, soar to its divine desire. *Hüzün* is, therefore, a sought-after state, and it is the absence, not the presence, of *hüzün* that causes the sufferer distress"[35]. Pamuk identifies the "mysterious air" of Istanbul as *hüzün* through Claude Lévi-Strauss's "*Tristesse*" term in his memoir, *Tristes Tropiques*. Similar to Istanbul's *hüzün*, Pamuk says *tristesse* is not a "pain" which "affects a solitary individual," but a "communal feeling, an atmosphere and a culture"[36]. Istanbul's *hüzün* is because of "ruins and of end-of-empire melancholy" in time "the world almost forgot that Istanbul existed"[37]. *Hüzün* is the melancholy of souls that hope to "act contrary to the dictates of society and the state, to be 'Eastern' when asked to be 'Western' and 'Western' when they were expected to be 'Eastern'"[38]. Pamuk approves that Hüzün rises out of the pain of impoverishment, but it does not belong to the outside observer. Pamuk defines the term Hüzün as a mutual melancholic feeling, an atmosphere and a shared culture through the tristesse that Lévi-Strauss contemplates the huddled masses and their wretched lives. Pamuk wrote, the tristesse that Lévi-Strauss mentions is a matter "a Westerner might feel as he surveys those vast poverty-stricken cities of the tropics, as he contemplates the huddled masses and their wretched lives."[39] As the Westerner observes the city differently, "Tristesse implies a guiltridden Westerner who seeks to assuage his pain by refusing to let cliché and prejudice color his impressions."[40]

In *Mourning and Melancholia*, Freud argued that responses to loss are "reaction to the loss of a loved object"[41], which takes place in the conscious

---

[33] *Ibid.*, 105
[34] *Ibid.*, 105
[35] Manguel 2005, 1
[36] Pamuk 2006b, 101
[37] *Ibid.*, 6
[38] *Ibid.*, 115
[39] *Ibid.*, 103
[40] *Ibid.*
[41] Freud 1976, 3043

mind. This melancholy ends with a loss of ego. During this period, in the world outside, the person loses meaning. Melancholia is not gloominess for a lost object, but it relates to the subject. In relation to the Ottoman Empire's reign, melancholia refers back to history's loss, not the Empire itself. This history is like a sign to show the true way by warning about mistakes the Ottoman Empire territory inhabitants have experienced in the past. Hande Gurses says that Istanbul's image is a picture of a "city filled with the presence of ruins that blur the boundary between the new and the old," which "embodies both sides of the binary opposition" and allows Pamuk to "discover the different Orhans alongside the different Istanbuls"[42]. This grey tone of Istanbul's black-and-white shades reflects how the city belongs to both East and West as the colours symbolize. The binary opposition of the Ottoman Empire's hope to show Istanbul as the centre of power and today's isolated position, reflects its grey tone, too. This grey tone of *hüzün* consists of all the inhabitants and acts as a mirror that displays residents' feelings toward their city and its glorious history.

---

[42] Afridi 2012, 52

Chapter 9
Easternization of World Literature

Adopting the Easternization thesis within the frame of literature is feasible through comparative studies. Easternization studies' resultant interaction in Western culture on the occasion of Eastern culture and literature is part of this cultural study. Literature should be understood as a social and communicative system because although culture is a wider concept than literature, literary texts play the main role in sorting out other civilizations' society, history, and culture as a whole. Literary studies, such as comparative studies, help in developing cultural subcategories. Analyzing the effects of Eastern literature on Western literature or the literary interactions of both seems possible with comparative studies such as comparative literature, which captures a wider range of literary works. Goethe began to speak and write about world literature in the 1820s, reflected in his statement, "National literature is now a rather unmeaning term; the epoch of world literature is at hand, and everyone must strive to hasten its approach"[1]. World literature is studied through the global growth of European and non-European literature, and Goethe's concept of *Weltliteratur* reflects the importance of non-Western-origin works as well as Western-oriented works. As Damrosch states in *What is World Literature?* nowadays world literature is the escape of national literature that enables writers in small countries to reach global audiences, and that helps worldwide readers to have a better sense of the world. Today, world literature reflects the best literature that each nation offers. Modern literature and the following contemporary postmodern literature, through combining elements of genre parody, pastiche, and intertextuality, gives an excellent opportunity to re-experience old-time masterpieces.

Irrespective of masterpieces, studying nations' produced literary texts looks impossible. At least research about the Eastern culture's capabilities outside of its magnificent old literary masterpieces is impossible. Discussing symptoms of Eastern- rooted cultural specifics in Western culture while neglecting Eastern literary masterpieces that reflect Eastern spirit and culture, looks absurd. David Damrosch quotes Ray Chow's colonial views toward literature and deduces a concept that "literature is strictly subordinated to a social Darwinian understanding of the nation: masterpieces correspond to

---

[1] Damrosch 2003, 1

master nations and master cultures"[2]. He marginalizes "others to the other that is the great Asian civilization" and continues: "The critique of Eurocentrism is to be thorough and fundamental, cannot take place at the level of replacing one set of texts with another set of texts. Rather, it must question the very assumption that nation-states with national languages are the only possible cultural formations that produce 'literature' [...] worth examining"[3]. He reminds us that the old Eurocentric models of language and literature study "being reproduced ad infinitum in non-European language and literature pedagogy" and predicts that "the active disabling of such reproduction of Eurocentrism-in-the-name-of-the-other," should be "one of comparative literature's foremost tasks in the future"[4] World Literature for David Damrosch is not a body of literature but a way of reading literature that makes our worldview. Edward Said emphasizes that to understand our multipolar world in comparative or contrapuntal perspective we need to "think through and interpret together experiences that are discrepant, each with its particular agenda and pace of development, its own internal formations, its internal coherence and system of external relationships, all of them coexisting and interacting with others"[5]. He thinks that scholar of comparative literature must "move beyond insularity and provincialism and to see several cultures and literatures together" beyond "reductive nationalism and uncritical dogma"[6]. He reminds us that the aim of comparative literature is to "see some son of whole instead of the defensive little patch offered by one's own culture, literature, and history"[7].

Historical, political, or economic inequalities, structure world literature. Because literary resources of nations have different origins and their writers' traditions are not equal, they form variously over time. These national works make up an evident heritage shared by all writers of the world. Pascale Casanova believes that all writers gather their literary past together to a competition of "national grouping," and they "reactivate" literary history "without even being conscious of it"[8]. This national and international history makes the writer who he is. Casanova thinks international literature has to struggle against national politics and international political forces simulta-

---

[2] Bernheimer 1995, 109
[3] *Ibid.*
[4] *Ibid.*
[5] Said 1993, 32
[6] *Ibid.*, 43
[7] *Ibid.*
[8] Casanova 2004, 40

neously. She thinks dominant powers define linguistic domination policies. Even nationally political independence is not enough to get free of publishing control and domination: "the world of letters is a relatively unified space characterized by the opposition between the great national literary spaces, which are also the oldest—and, the best endowed—and those literary spaces that have more recently appeared and that are poor by comparison"[9]. For Casanova, both dominated and dominant literatures are dependent, but politically strong newer literatures sometimes dominate older ones through culture and language. Thus, national writers should be aware of the international literary system and its revolutions instead of considering only the local norms and political chronologies. Awareness of the present global literature "allows us to sketch the structure of the literary field in space and time, or, better perhaps, in a time that has become space"[10]. The homology between international and national literary spaces is the product of a progressive unification; thus, the international field "tends toward greater autonomy through the emergence of autonomous sub-poles in each national space."[11]

Comparative literature is a hybrid, and as Haun Saussy asserts, "hybridity as such often becomes a one-size-fits-all term good for blotting out specific interactions"[12]. Damrosch's point of view about world literature is practical. Particularly, Literary Easternization analyzes the Easternization process of mutual effect between literary outputs, and Damrosch says: "world literature is always as much about the host culture's values and needs as it is about a work's source culture"[13]. He thinks these dealings are "double refraction" in which both the host and the source cultures "providing the two foci that generate the elliptical space within which a work lives as world literature, connected to both cultures, circumscribed by neither alone"[14]. Damrosch's definition of world literature precisely identifies the Easternization thesis from a literary perspective although defining comparative literature in the same territory is indistinguishable from Damrosch's perspective. Comparative literature includes translation, globalization, migration and exile, and world literature. It needs to redefine its identity in the twenty-first century through literary-cultural bonds of Eastern and Western parts of the globe. Comparative literature provides an opportunity for new comparatists to

---

[9] *Ibid.*, 83
[10] *Ibid.*, 101
[11] *Ibid.*, 109
[12] Saussy 2006, 29
[13] Damrosch 2003, 283
[14] *Ibid.*, 283

interpret old books based on social and political issues of the time, as it involves historicism and presentism. As Bernheimer asserts, literature intrinsically is "mixed, stereophonic, porous, marked by exchanges and influences, international"[15]. Bernheimer says that comparative literature is "inherently pluralist" and its "international perspective remarks the entire deck, reconceives not only the individual text but the international corpus, makes it possible to discern kinships and allegiances and patterns that are invisible to the national literature scholar, of whatever stripe he or she may be"[16]. In the same vein, Saussy thinks that the history of comparative literature is restricted by the disciplines of the humanities. Radical views make it impossible to define a world and the realms of comparative literature's territory. He says "this is not just an impossibility but an impossibility that institutes literature and the reading of literature as the medium in which the possibilities of humanities is to be defined and redefined and re-redefined again precisely because, at its core, it preserves its impossibility like a talisman ensuring its future, ensuring that it can always be compared"[17]. There is an urge for comparative literature to leave its traditional Eurocentric perspective and turn toward a global outlook hugging Western cultures and non-Western other cultural discourses based on cross-cultural contacts and hybridity. Saussy thinks "comparative francophone, ethnic, and minority studies can be such an antidote to cultural nationalism and to the theoretical generalizations that lead to an unnecessary opposition between knowledge and culture or theory and literature"[18].

The territory of comparative literature for comparatist Claudio Guillén is supernatural. Supernaturality extends or transcends the established borders of literature. It extends influence held by separate nations and eliminates questions of inequality, influence, or the West and the rest. Guillén defines three models of supranationality and chooses the third model to describe his ideas. Exceeding Cultural, historical, or linguistic resemblances, he thinks today's East-West studies offer opportunities for resolving problems: "as the framework evolves, a contrary motion can begin, and new knowledge or some unpublished facts can challenge any theoretical notion [that] permits the dialogue between unity and diversity that stimulates comparativism"[19]. For him, supranational assets are based on principles of the theory of literature.

---

[15] Bernheimer 1995, 79
[16] *Ibid.*
[17] Saussy 2006, 93
[18] *Ibid.*, 105
[19] Guilleń 1993, 70

Thus, East-West studies under supranatural perspective are beyond traditional Eurocentric considerations. Comparative literature can overcome the orders of national language and literature. Haun Saussy thinks that the struggle between Eurocentric and non-Western theory is similar to the struggle between literature and cultural studies. He asserts that during this conflict, "the front line dissolves and the opposing forces melt into one another"[20]. Thus, the integration of non-Western texts into comparative literature provides a new Eurocentric class of literature that does not assure a vision of the remote cultures' canon but captures their traditions and specialities. "Comparative literature has always thought about the difference, but inequality remains foreign to its usual vocabulary, transverse to its standing organization of differences"[21]. Pamuk addresses his basic feeling by telling that he never found himself in the centre of the world. He asserts, like most people in the world "there was a world literature, and its center, too, was very far away from me."[22] He says, "what I had in mind was Western, not world, literature, and we Turks were outside it."[23] He thinks writing and reading is like "leaving one world to find consolation in the other world's otherness, the strange and the wondrous."[24]

According to Halide Edib, "The spread of literacy is not an absolute end in itself, for an increase in the number of those who can merely read is not an increase in the number of educated people. It is not desirable for us to disown the Persian and Arabic influences in our culture; we have neither been Persianized nor Arabicized by them"[25]. After Naguib Mahfuz, Abdulrahman Munif, and Emil Habibi, snippy writers of Eastern identity from Muslim countries got a poor response from international audiences. But Pamuk reminds us that "Turks were never colonized by a world power, [and] 'worshipping Europe' or 'imitating the West' has never carried the damning, humiliating overtones described by Frantz Fanon, V.S. Naipaul, or Edward Said"[26]. Pamuk watches his nation from an objective point of view to distance himself and his nation. He once said, "I've been saying to my readers that what is important is not clash of parties, civilizations, cultures, East and West, whatever. But think that other peoples in other continents and civilizations

---

[20] Saussy 2006, 22
[21] *Ibid.*, 28
[22] Pamuk 2007, 410
[23] Ibid.
[24] *Ibid.*
[25] Edib 1935, 164
[26] Pamuk 2011a, 1

are actually exactly like you and you can learn this through literature. Pay attention to good literature and novels, and do not believe in politicians"[27]. Pamuk believes that accepting of the clash from the West and the East is wrong. He tries to turn around this and asserts "all generalizations about East and West are generalizations. Don't believe them, don't buy them."[28] He thinks even if the generalized East and West exist, but "if you believe them too much, then you are paving the way for war."[29] He tells about Turkey, where "destroyed its democracy in years because its intellectuals, its media, its press believed in, too much, in the westness of West and the eastness of East."[30]

Pamuk criticized the former President of the United States, George W. Bush because he "put a lot of distance between East and West" with his Middle-East war adventure[31]. He thinks Bush made Islamic countries angry with the United States and the West, to "raise the tension between East and West"[32]; "in my books, I always looked for a sort of harmony between the so-called East and West. In short, what I wrote in my books for years was misquoted, and used as a sort of apology for what had been done. And what had been done was a cruel thing"[33]. "You go to the past and try to invent a pure image of yourself, then you understand the vanity and romanticism of it. Then you go to the West and are shamelessly inspired by the newest postmodern form. Then you also realize the vanity of it. And your pendulum goes back between East and West"[34]. Pamuk thinks novelists write of others' lives as their own lives and it helps them to change the boundaries of their identities. Pamuk, as a novelist, says, "Others become 'us' and we become 'others.' Certainly, a novel can achieve both feats simultaneously. Even as it describes our own lives as if they were the lives of others, it offers us the chance to describe other people's lives as if they were our own"[35]. Talât Halman wrote: "The narrator pushed into an absence of identity, recognizes a textual space where Self might become Other, or vice versa, where neither are repressed, or, in Jalaladdin Rumi's phrasing, where the line 'So I am you!' is imminent"[36].

---

[27] Pamuk 2002, 1
[28] *Ibid.*
[29] *Ibid.*
[30] *Ibid.*
[31] Pamuk 2004, 1
[32] *Ibid.*
[33] *Ibid.*
[34] Lavery 2003, 1
[35] Pamuk 2007, 228
[36] Halman 2010, 133

Reflexivity refers to circular relationships between cause and effect and how they affect one another: also, how someone's ideas and thoughts are inherently biased and reflected in their social lives. Existing Oriental roots in Occidentalism show that Western imagination not only captures what it owns but also what the East owns and the West lacks. Romanticism and Exoticism are examples in Western society that is interested in non-Western works. Besides, the mirror stage is a concept in the psychoanalytic theory of Jacques Lacan in which, from 6 to 18 months, infants recognize themselves in a mirror as an independent individual like his mother. The infant who is not able to coordinate his body finds an unfragmented and complete body in the mirror and identifies himself. This flawless image is our ego. Exoticism is a way of seeing "the Other" from the Western viewpoint of the East. Exoticism is an interest to see in a different way or a different kind of representation in which we change Western views and embodiments in ourselves. It has roots in Said's *Orientalism* or acts as a genre of Orientalism, with roots in the second half of the eighteenth century in Europe. As a kind of cultural relativism like nationalism, Exoticism is a kind of *Orientalism*. Edward Said in *Covering Islam* reminds us of how this exotic bitterness would be pleasant for Western media. Exoticism or Orientalism is a doubled Orientalism. This duplication of discourse ends in a semantic ambiguity in the leading text. In an exotic text, we look at a strange creature, and this strangeness looks natural. Thus, we confront a kind of myth, and that expresses a new identity or claims to do so.

Also, Bhabha states that the discourse of mimicry reflects "ambivalence," and continually must produce "its slippage, its excess, its difference"[37]. European writers were inspired by Middle Eastern stories expounded by merchants and armies of the Crusades. Therefore, travellers and their works had a high impact on the shape of world literature. These stories inspired French writer Jean de La Fontaine's *Fables*, Montesquieu's *Persian Letters*, Victor Hugo's *Les Orientales*, Spanish Miguel de Cervantes *Don Quixote*, Petrus Alphonso's *Disciplina Clericalis*, Don Juan Manuel's *Tales of Count Lucanor*, German Hugo von Hofmannsthal's *The Tale of the 672 Nights*, and Johann Wolfgang von Goethe's *West-Eastern Diwan*; all of these works introduced Eastern adventures to Western readers[38]. Inspired by the fantastic stories such as *One Thousand and One Nights*, Europeans produced more memorable stories such as *Robinson Crusoe* and *Gulliver's Travels* [39]. Despite

---

[37] Bhabha 1994, 122
[38] Neda 2004, 273-97
[39] *Ibid.*, 281

the origins of the novel from Classical Greece and Rome, the New Age Movement with Eastern roots is found in novels.

Independent from Said's discourse, historical *Orientalism* had a concrete reality accepted by Westerners involved in Oriental implementation. Said's notion of *Orientalism* does not fit the historical situation in territory that was Eurocentrically called the Middle East or even semi-European Turkey. Pamuk asserts that through military and economic comparisons Western dominance over Islam and "the East as a whole"[40] is shown. Mahnaz Afridi writes, "The relentless contact and exchange between […] opposing orientations have blended and saturated into the same, to the degree that difference is no longer recognizable"[41]. Edward Said found any novel as a discovery process that follows a tension in the heart of the narrative designated as authority and molestation. Authority is the will to power and the continuity it brings about. Molestation is the responsibility and difficulty the authority has to face. "Molestation, then, is a consciousness of one's duplicity, one's confinement to a fictive, scriptive realm, whether one is a character or a novelist. And molestation occurs when novelists and critics traditionally remind themselves of how the novel is always subject to a comparison with reality and thereby found to be illusion"[42]. Thus, Said thinks that because of restrictions in fiction to reflect a real world, a novelist's great problem is to create realistic and believable characters. Edward Said mentioned that "knowledge of other cultures" is a necessary element in the "circumstances of interpretation"[43] for two reasons: first, the researcher should feel that he is "answerable to and in uncoercive contact with the culture"[44]. Second, for interpretation that Said calls "the state of knowledge by various means," we need "intellectual" as well as "social" and "political" knowledge of interpretation[45]. Just the same he stressed, "knowledge of the social world […] is always no better than the interpretations on which it is based"[46].

In Pamuk's *The White Castle* Hoja and the Venetian start to "search together, discover together, progress together"[47]. The Italian says, "I must convince myself that the uncanny resemblance between us was a blunder of memory, a

---

[40] Pamuk 2006a, 157
[41] Afridi 2012, 4
[42] Said 1985, 84
[43] Said 1997, 163
[44] *ibid.*
[45] *Ibid.*, 164
[46] *Ibid.*, 168
[47] Pamuk 2009, 23

bitter illusion that should be forgotten"[48]. Elsewhere he says, "I didn't even want to learn the identity of this other person I was inside of"[49]. The Venetian remembers, "Because he talked about 'our' plans, 'our' future, I happily went along with him"[50]. "I began to believe that my personality had split itself off from me and united with Hoja's, and vice versa"[51]. The Italian says, "by searching for the strange within ourselves, we, too, would become someone else"[52]. Likewise, in *My Name is Red*, Black believes in the meeting of East and West and in *The Blak Book*, Galip confesses that he lived to imitate Jalal and to come closer to him through imitation; in the hope that that one day he might become one with him, or learn to live as "He did"[53].

There are no longer Western but worldwide scientific movements. I think it is not necessary anymore to compare the Middle-Eastern contributions with that of other non-Western regions or even with its own past record. Categorizing Oriental languages such as Arabic as a dead language and European languages such as English as living is a great mistake and the main characteristic of the Oriental mentality. During the period of Western impact on the Middle East, the Western verbal culture was accepted and internalized by Easterners, and Western novels were translated and Western literary forms thoroughly assimilated. Morson wrote that "Our concept of the novel is likely to change: the westernization of the East means the easternization of the Western genre"[54]. Morson describes problems that the Easternization of the Western genre brings about. He says "when something is borrowed it is changed"[55]. From a formalistic point of view, he mentions that what is borrowed in the process of translation or imitation, changes. Because these works are torn from their native land, they deceive us about their completeness as a genre and lose their place in literary-cultural debates of the time. Indeed, they get "canons and traditions of their new homeland. The same text, therefore, becomes, in effect, a different work; read in terms of a new hierarchy of literary functions, it comes to serve new functions"[56]. He continues, "The more central a literary fact the new work becomes, the more will the system have to change in order to assimilate it. The work is always

---

[48] *Ibid.*, 77
[49] *Ibid.*, 86
[50] *Ibid.*, 96
[51] *Ibid.*, 102
[52] *Ibid.*, 139
[53] Pamuk 2006a, 118
[54] Morson 1979, 130
[55] *Ibid.*, 130
[56] *Ibid.*, 130-31

imported as a foreign product, and some awareness of its different significance in a different literary system will always be present."[57]

Decades earlier Tanpınar said, "We shall enter the world concert with our national identity"[58]. Pamuk says the authors who expected to be Western but are not able to "cleanse themselves of their traditional identities," had to "set out on an irreversible journey to the twilit place between East and West"[59]. World literature does not categorize novels in binary terms as fantastic-realistic, high literary-popular, or Eastern-Western anymore. It does not aim to categorize the books, but to make a dialogue between them to "gain deeper clarification"[60]. Talât Halman asserted that "Turkish authors have squeezed into half a century virtually the entire experience of European, American, and Latin American fiction. Their achievement is remarkable because although emulating that monumental legacy, they have also been able to avoid imitation and to endow their works with an authentic Turkish personality"[61]. He declared, "Following many decades of conscious experimentation, questing for new values, acquisition of deeper literary and human insights, and stronger expertise in blending form and content, Turkish authors are creating an authentic synthesis of national and universal elements"[62]. Pamuk says, "My world is a mixture of the local—the national—and the West"[63]. Turkish literature, against its past that never was wide-ranging, looks forward to its future as a great face of world literature by giving more profound literary and human visions by blending national and universal elements. The history of literature in the Modern period in Europe begins with the Age of Enlightenment, and in Ottoman Turkey with social, cultural, and literary developments during the Tanzimat reforms, which aimed to mix non-Muslims and non-Turks into Ottoman society by increasing their civil rights and bringing equality. The literary output of this period resulted in literary genres that reflect the tension between Eastern and Western values. Being prone to Eastern and Turkish values was known as Alaturka, and a Western slant was defined as Alafranga. Stress on prose from the Tanzimat to contemporary literature clearly mirrors contemporary Turkish literary inclination to the novel. Master novelists such as Orhan Pamuk, Yaşar Kemal,

---

[57] Morson 1979, 130-31
[58] Seyhan 2008, 16
[59] Pamuk 2006b, 169
[60] Seyhan 2008, 203
[61] Halman 2011, 135
[62] *Ibid.*, 135
[63] Pamuk 2007, 410

Oğuz Atay, Ahmet Hamdi Tanpınar, Aziz Nesin, Zülfü Livaneli, Sabahattin Ali, Halit Ziya Uşaklıgil, Orhan Kemal, Yusuf Atılgan, Yahya Kemal, and Elif Şafak are the outcome of this enterprise.

Chapter 10

Intertextuality Represents Literary Easternization

Pamuk's works are full of quotes from different Eastern cultural centres through intertextual techniques. Literary Easternization in Pamuk's works is definable through intertextuality. The interpretation of Literary Easternization in Pamuk's works is not possible through the "hermeneutics of recovery" defined by Dilthey. As we investigate the effects of Easternization on Westerners through Eastern cultural worldviews, Literary Easternization, is the process of investigating how a text is received by its contemporary readers. The hermeneutics of recovery presupposes that the task of social inquiry is to reflect the original intention or meaning that motivates social action. However, Easternization does not presuppose that there is an original intended meaning that determines social behaviour, such as showing interest in Sufism as an Eastern worldview; it only asks questions based on evidence of whether recently increasing interest in Eastern-oriented literary works in the West is a consequence of acculturation adaptations of *both* East and West: Literary Easternization, for example, probes cited stories of Sufis, courtly loves, and also fairy tales similar to Chivalric romances narrated in Eastern courts, which draws Western readers' attention to Pamuk's novels such as *My Name is Red* or *The Black Book*. Clarifying such a confirmation is possible through *logoteunison*, which emphasizes that all literary works are in compliance with each other. Being affected by Eastern-oriented literary masterpieces reflected in a Western-style writer like Pamuk is a good example of *logoteunison* and literary adaptation of East and West. Pamuk uses appropriate intertextuality to show connections of Western and Eastern cultural fusion in making world literature. Intertextuality plays a big role in Pamuk's works as coordinating literary conjunction of old and contemporary, and East and West.

Before discussing the reasons and techniques of Pamuk's use of intertextuality, we need to look at the theory of intertextuality itself to find out what he took from this theory. As human beings, we confront the pastiche worlds of others, with their repetition, continuation, imitation, or alteration based on pre-existing backgrounds without any beginning. This sort of intertextuality is based upon the principle that older pre-texts become foundations for new texts. It means no text can be produced without prior fantastic or factual material so that creativity and innovation are always close to previous notions. This principle is at the root of developments in science and thought such as cosmology, philosophy, sociology, and linguistics. "'Intertextuality' thus breaks down old boundaries in which the 'text' in 'intertextuality' "delimits its methodologies to those of reading words (textuality), such as literature, history, philosophy," so that one can "envisage 'text' as any sign system" and thus realize that "there can be no outside of the text if language is its paradigm"[1]. Again, intertextuality is always rooted in previous texts. Even Aristotelian or Platonic imitation is not considered as "imitation of nature. In the case of Platonic imitation, the 'poet' always copies an earlier act of creation, which is itself already a copy [...]. From the perspective of Longinus, [...] Plato is asserting the superiority of his form of creation to that of [...] beloved Homer"[2]. Intertextuality accepts that text is influenced by other texts, and as a result, there is no final source. There is a generational conflict in the concepts of influence and intertextuality in such a way that "to many people, influence has smacked of elitism" and "influence should refer to relation built on dyads of transmission from one unity (author, work, tradition) to another."[3] The shape of intertextuality and influence are interrelated, and like Americans who have used the term intertextuality in a context of enlargement, intertextuality may have seen as "the enlargement of a familiar idea or as an entirely new concept to replace the outmoded notion of influence."[4]

Intertextuality provides a polysomic and dynamic text. Mary Orr in *Intertextuality* claims, "Texts are the production of multiple agencies and a plethora of intentions, from pleasure to instruction, exemplification to enlightenment. The contexts of influence and the influences of context are therefore the 'how' and 'why' questions any text will variously address, even if it is concerned primarily with form or a language game"[5]. The difference between discovery and invention is that some matters seem so clear that people take them for granted, but when someone notices them, everyone asks himself about the importance of such simple and clear discoveries. "Interpretation is shaped by a complex of relations between the text, the reader, writing, printing, polishing, and history: the history that is inscribed in the language of the text and in the history that is carried in the reader's reading. Such a history has been given a name: intertextuality"[6]. Either, intertextuality is "used to signify the

---

[1] Orr 2003, 45
[2] Worton 1990, 3
[3] Clayton 1991, 3-4
[4] *Ibid.*
[5] Orr 2003, 84
[6] Plottel 1978, xx

multiple ways in which any literary text is inseparably inter-involved with other texts, whether by its open or covert citations or, allusions or by its assimilation of the formal and substantive features of an earlier text or texts"[7].

Intertextuality is one of the great discoveries of the twentieth century that brought a new perspective to the elements of texts. It is a mirror that reflects new texts in previous writers. "The theory of intertextuality insists that a text [...] cannot exist as a hermetic or self-sufficient whole, and so does not function as a closed system"[8]. Classical textual structuralism was unable to answer such questions: the text was considered a closed and self-sufficient phenomenon and the author, status, time, location, and culture were not so important to be analyzed. Even history was defined by the intertextual relations of intergenerational experiences. Intertextuality as deconstruction and différance is "akin to such terms as 'the imagination,' 'history' or 'postmodernism'" and thus makes a "set of critical procedures for interpretation"[9]. It brought a new vision to create post-structuralism. Post-structuralist theorists "attempt to disrupt notions of stable meaning and objective interpretation"[10]. Actually, Intertextuality "is the oldest troping we know, the most ancient textual (con)figuration, its presence as a specific form of attention may be located within the loose amalgamation of poststructuralist critical theories"[11].

Mikhail Bakhtin's ideas played a pivotal role in the creation of intertextuality. "Bakhtin confronted at least three dominant movements in his time—movements attributed to linguists, formalists, and literary critics—all of which, despite their differences, shared common views on textual studies. Bakhtin believed in the hyper-linguistic and intertextual relations, specifically social hypertexts, and knew that they had a significant effect on literary texts"[12]. Also, Bulgarian-French philosopher, literary critic, psychoanalyst, and sociologist Julia Kristeva, using the Prague school of Russian Formalism theories of dialogism and polyphony, created new words and terminologies for this new movement of social sciences and created a new perspective in art and literature studies. Formalism, linguistics, semiotics, and comparative mythology and procedures such as structuralism and post-structuralism interact with intertextuality. Kristeva used Bakhtin's theories and Saussurian linguistics, even as Roland Barthes used Gaston Bachelard's theories. Michael

---

[7] Abrams 1993, 285
[8] Worton 1990, 1
[9] Allen 2000, 2
[10] *Ibid.*, 3
[11] O'Donnell 1989, xiii
[12] Motlagh 2008a, 397

Riffaterre used structuralism and formalistic analysis, while Laurent Jenny tends toward philosophical issues. Actually, "While these reiterations certainly clarify and refine various aspects of intertextuality, they also tacitly exclude alternative theories or positions that might challenge (their own) pre-given dispositions of viewpoint, appraisal and methodological approach"[13]. However, intertextuality groups can be classified into parts that insist on the theory, and others that insist on usage. Kristeva's manifesto-like essay, "Word, dialog, novel," the fourth chapter of *Semiotike*, in the study of Bakhtin's work on dialogue and carnival, defines intertextuality: any text is "a mosaic of quotations; any text is the absorption and transformation of another"[14]. This means that a text is a mosaic of quotations or references to other texts in an open system of dialogue with other texts. Thus, intertextuality takes the place of intersubjectivity. Kristeva believes a text is constructed not from an original mind but from a compilation of known discourses. She wrote that the text is "a productivity, and this means: first, that its relationship to the language in which it is situated is redistributive (destructive-constructive), and hence can be better approached through logical categories rather than linguistic ones, and second, that it is a permutation of texts, an intertextuality: in the space of a given text, several utterances, taken from other texts, intersect and neutralize one another"[15].

Kristeva says "imitation and translation should also be considered as forms of creative splitting or catastrophe which function both as temporary proofs of the integrity of the writing subject and as transgressive inscriptions of fluidity into textuality"[16], which means texts obtain their meaning from social and literary systems more than the physical world. Kristeva and Bakhtin wrote that "texts cannot be separated from the larger cultural or social textuality out of which they are constructed. All texts, therefore, contain within them the ideological structures and struggles expressed in society through discourse"[17]. Bakhtin believes in polyphony, metalanguage, and dialogue in the study of literary works, and he criticizes linguistics and stylistics because they relate to people, and the studies that relate to humankind must be based on dialogue. He even believes that philosophical theories must support traditions and social life. Bakhtin notices social relations and their effect on humanity. He praises the novel because more

---

[13] Orr 2003, 7
[14] Kristeva 1980, 66
[15] *Ibid.*, 36
[16] Worton 1990, 9
[17] Allen 2000, 36

convergence and integration take place in it than in other literary genres. In the novel, there is something to tell and someone to affect the society and culture of humanity. Every character in this dialogic novel has a particular and unique "personality" that "involves that character's world-view, the typical mode of speech, ideological and social positioning, all of which are expressed through the character's words. Bakhtin speaks of characters as expressing an idea or 'world-view' and of the image of voice associated with that character's consciousness"[18]. For Bakhtin, the author does not create a character, "but rather the hero's discourse is about himself and his world"[19]. For him, culture and history are texts that combine with the author, but the sciences like psychology or linguistics that distinguish between text and society are worthless. Bakhtin's "heteroglossia" that he describes in *The Dialogic Imagination* means "double voiced" in Greek [20]. Even for Kristeva, the subject is double because "the words that [the] subject utters are intertextual (clichéd, already written), and the pronominal signifiers which refer to that subject are always changing and have no stable signified ('outside' subject) to which they can be referred"[21]. Oswald Ducrot in *Le dire et le dit* (1984) says that in Bakhtin's thought "there are a group of texts and especially literary texts that should consider this particular that some voices should talk at the same time without being better than the other one and provide refuge for the others. The matter is that, against classical or formal literature, there is popular or carnivalesque literature"[22].

Kristeva's cooperation with Roland Barthes, Michel Foucault, Philippe Sollers and Jacques Derrida in the *Tel Quel* literary magazine, attending Jacques Lacan's classes, and being influenced by Bakhtin, Claude Lévi-Strauss, Saussure, and Freud helped her to define intertextuality in an article titled "Le mot, le dialog, le roman" in 1966. Against Bakhtin, who criticizes formalists, she focuses on the text itself. The most problematic aspect of Kristeva's theory is its superficiality: she does not try to prove her ideas because she does not restrict the intertextuality of any text since she finds all texts as abstract and subjective. Accepting this intertextual concept of the relation between all texts is not applicable in criticism. In *The Pleasure of the Text*, Roland Barthes defines "inter-text" as "the impossibility of living outside

---

[18] *Ibid.*, 23
[19] Bakhtin 1984, 23
[20] Bakhtin 1982, 295
[21] Allen 2000, 43
[22] Motlagh 2012, 85

the infinite text [...] the book creates meaning, the meaning creates the life"[23]. His intertextuality "has less to do with specific inter-texts than with the entire cultural code, comprised, as it is, of discourses, stereotypes, clichés, and ways of saying. Intertextuality, viewed in this way, means that for Barthes, as for Derrida, 'nothing exists outside the text'; text here meaning the intertextual"[24]. For Barthes, there are no original texts. In 1973 Barthes described intertextuality in the *Encyclopedie universalis*: "The text is productivity. Not in the sense that it is a product of being worked (as narrative technique or the mastery of style would demand), but as the very theatre of a production where the producer of the text and the reader come together."[25] He continued, even in written fixed form, the text works and does not stop working, or undertaking a process of production. The text "deconstructs the language of communication, representation or expression" and "reconstructs another language."[26] He wrote that every text is an intertext and other texts are present within it: "Fragments of codes, formulae, model rhythms, bits of social discourse pass into the text and are redistributed within it."[27]

For Barthes, texts and works are different elements: "A work is a finished object, something computable, which can occupy a physical space," but the text is a methodological field, which means "The work is held in the hand, the text in language"[28]. For him, "The 'text' is that which is potentially released within a 'work' and yet that which exists between that text and other texts. It is intertextual to the core and [...] it foregrounds dramatically the productive role of the reader"[29]. He wrote, "The plural of the Text depends [...] not on the ambiguity of its contents but on what might be called the stereographic plurality"[30]. This plurality of discourse meanings relates to the theory of text and as a result, intertextuality. However, Kristeva's intertextuality "has nothing to do with influence, sources, or even the stabilized model favoured in historical work of 'text' and 'context.' In this model, 'context' might explain 'text' but remains, ultimately, distinct from it"[31]. The similarities of Barthes and Kristeva's ideas are in showing importance to text and intertextuality. Intertextuality frees the text from imitation, frees one text from another one,

---

[23] Barthes 1975, 36
[24] Allen 2000, 74
[25] Orr 2003, 33
[26] *Ibid.*
[27] *Ibid.*
[28] Allen 2000, 66
[29] *Ibid.*, 68-69
[30] Barthes 1977, 159
[31] Allen 2000, 69

and increases creativity in production. But even before Kristeva and her definition of intertextuality, Barthes used the same term under the title of "*cryptogram*". He explained that any written trace precipitates, "as inside a chemical at first transparent, innocent and neutral, mere duration gradually reveals in suspension a whole past of increasing density, like a cryptogram"[32].

Barthes, as a well-known post-structuralist, supports important theories. He defines "zero degree of writing" in which, the reason for studying the text is for sensation and pleasure, but finally one becomes alone with the final sense that the text does not express, which is an enigma. For him, texts change in complex communication that results in the dynamism of the text. Barthes' term "The Death of the Author" in *Image, Music, Text* announces that the text is a contexture of quotations that come from cultural centres. By the death of the Author, a new reader is born who in a new time and place defines a new meaning and interpretation that the Author could not predict. Barthes explained that text is made of various writings mixed with dialogue, parody, contestation, and drawn from many cultures and this multiplicity is focused on the reader, not the author. Thus, a text's unity lies not in its origin but in its not personal destination: "the reader is without history, biography, psychology; he is simply that someone who holds together in a single field all the traces by which the written text is constituted [...] the birth of the reader must be at the cost of the death of the Author."[33]

Neither Barthes nor Kristeva ever devoted any article to intertextuality. At first, the term intertextuality was used seven times by Barthes in different studies and conferences from 1969 up to 1975 [34]. The similarities of Barthes's and Kristeva's ideas are that both of them do not try to find the effects of any text on the other(s). Intertextuality for Barthes is more complicated than a simple study of quotations; it becomes a complicated matter, which distinguishes between text and intertext. As mentioned, intertextuality does not restrict criticism to a few texts that influence the writer, but to texts that help in *reading* it. He accepts everything that can relate to the text. Even readers have a significant influence on creativity. Readers and text are connected in the text. Studying the same text at different times creates two different intertextual views. This process ends with Barthes' movement from structuralism to post-structuralism.

---

[32] Barthes 1984, 23
[33] Barthes 1977, 75
[34] Motlagh 2012, 176-77

Riffaterre, in *Text Production*, asserts that "the text refers not to objects outside of itself, but to an inter-text. The words of the text signify not by referring to things, but by presupposing other texts"[35]. The difference between him and other intertextuality researchers is that instead of moving "outwards from the text to what we have called the general or social text and so [to] explode the traditional idea of textual unity," "Riffaterre reads in a backwards movement, from text to textual invariant, from mimetic ungrammaticalities to semiotic (textual) unity"[36]. For him, intertextuality is an excessive statue and differs for different people during the reading of the text. Thus, the reader is the most crucial element in defining intertextuality, and it seems that his ideas are closer to Barthes than to Kristeva. Intertextuality is between text and intertext, and if intertextuality is impaired, the text loses its reasonableness during that time. For Riffaterre and Kristeva, a text is a closed unit that defined in an intertextual process.

Laurent Jenny "distinguishes between works which are explicitly intertextual – such as imitations, parodies, citations, montages and plagiarisms – and those works in which the intertextual relation is not foregrounded"[37]. He criticizes intertextuality because it is rusty and overused. He does not use intertextuality excessively as Kristeva does. He does not accept a mosaic system of quotations and the excessive meaning of texts. In *Semiotique du collage intertextual, ou la literature a coups de ciseaux in collages* (1978), polyphony and dialogue are the result of the presence of heterogeneous elements in a text.

Against Kristeva and Barthes, Bloom does not "accept social and cultural contexts as relevant intertextual fields of meaning for literary texts. For Bloom, literary texts can only have other specific literary texts as inter-texts"[38]. He believes "there are no texts, but only relationships between texts. These relationships depend upon a critical act, a misreading or misprision"[39]. For him, "all reading is misreading because of the anxiety of influence, or all reading is misreading because of the inability of readers to draw a verifiable frame around the intertextual domain within which texts exist and signify and to distinguish relevant from irrelevant inter-texts"[40]. The similarity of his idea

---

[35] Riffaterre 1980, 228
[36] Allen 2000, 124-25
[37] *Ibid.*, 113
[38] *Ibid.*, 140-41
[39] Bloom 1975, 71
[40] Allen 2000, 140

with Kristeva is in the idea that "intertextuality involves the transposition of elements from existent systems into new signifying relations"[41].

Genette redefined Barthes and Kristeva's intertextuality as the five-branched hypertextuality, intertextuality, paratextuality, transtextuality, and metatextuality. His study contains semiotics and (post)structuralism, which help him to study intertext and relations of texts with others in detail. He studies the affection of two texts on different levels. In *Palimpsestes* (1997) Genette defines intertextuality as the relation between the two texts. Normal aspects happen when a part of the text appears in another text. He explains that the other text's writer does not want to hide the first writer's text, and therefore shows them in quotation marks. Another aspect of Genette's intertextuality is plagiarism, in which the writer hides the source of a written text. Also, sometimes a text's writer does not want to hide the original text and gives signs to identify the source of a text through allusions, allegories, and ironies. For him, Intertextuality and Transtextuality is the study of the connection of text to the related hypertext. "Reading Kristeva's notion of intertextuality as referring to the literal and effective presence in a text of another text, he asserts that intertextuality is an inadequate term and proposes in its place "transtextuality" (or textual transcendence), by which he means everything, be it explicit or latent, that links one text to others which is how we in this volume understand and use the term intertextuality"[42]. Paratextuality investigates the relationship of text with other connected or separate texts or "the relations between the body of a text and its titles, epigraphs, illustrations, notes, first drafts, etc."[43]. For him, texts are always in the cover of other texts, which he calls paratexts, which are not recognizable from the main text and must be passed to reach the main text. Briefly, paratexts are a combination of intertexts and outer texts. Metatextuality studies the analytical elevation of text in respect to another one through interpretation and paraphrasing that, without any quotation, criticizes and interprets another text in a positive or negative way. Architextuality probes the relationship between the reader and the characters of tragedy (epic), comedy (parody) or between a text and the text of its kind and "now defined as a tacit, perhaps even unconscious, gesture to genre demarcations"[44]. Hypertextuality "is a practice which includes and informs all literary genres, and he goes so far as to assert that the hypertext necessarily gains in some

---

[41] *Ibid.*, 113
[42] Worton 1990, 22
[43] *Ibid.*
[44] Worton 1990, 22-23

way or another from the reader's awareness of its signifying and determining relationship with its hypertext(s)"[45], and studies the relationship between two artistic texts based on the overall effect and inspiration of retrieves. He means the creation of the other text without the first one is impossible in this way because derivation as transformational (parody, travesty, transposition) and imitational (pastiche, caricature, forgery) plays the leading role in this kind.

Orhan Pamuk uses a stream of consciousness, intertextuality, metafiction, irony, supplementation, allegory, and palimpsest techniques masterfully. He is a well-known artisan of postmodern intertextuality. His use of Intertextuality includes quotation, adaptation, allusion, and parody. Postmodern fiction extended its borders to history and historical discourse—or as Edward Said says, it includes the world. This world of stories is a community's cultural assets, and postmodern techniques create experimental intertextual worlds. Postmodernism provides some basic techniques to write unique books, and intertextuality is one of them. Most of the postmodern novels written in Turkey use a fictional structure from Western novels and form a bond with the traditions of the society where these novels are born. Being inspired is among the requirements of intertextuality. Some critics believe that there is no question of plagiarism in postmodern literature. Also, during literary history, writers in the context of mimesis were influenced by other poets and authors through inspiration, influence, imitation, or plagiarism. Because there is no framework for these terms, the intertextuality of postmodernism covers a wide range of interpretations. Based on the theory, there are a limited number of stories in the world, and world literature uses these stories. The critical matter is to add personal ideas in retelling the stories. Intertextuality refers to the traces of other texts in the text. It has a prominent place in Turkish literature as in much world literature. Pamuk is among the most popular writers who use intertextuality theory. He refers to literary sources from East and West. Some of Orhan Pamuk's works are influenced by and quote works of other writers, which Pamuk almost always uses in his novels in full disclosure. When the honorary doctorate was awarded to Pamuk by the Freie University of Berlin, they announced on their website that they honoured him because "in a subtle and questioning manner, Orhan Pamuk's narratives, including the use of intertextual and intermedial techniques, establish the question of Turkish identity as a theme. He succeeds in uniting Eastern narrative traditions and their theoretical reflection with Western narrative traditions and literary theory."

---

[45] *Ibid.*, 23

Several times Pamuk has been criticized for plagiarism. Critics have mentioned resemblances of *Snow* with Fyodor Dostoyevsky's *Demons* (1872), *My Name is Red* to Umberto Eco's *The Name of the Rose* (1983), and *The White Castle* to *Kanuni devrinde Istanbul* [*Istanbul at the Time of Kanuni*] (1964). This is why Pamuk defends his 'collage book' (*The Black Book*). Despite attacks of Turkish critics against Pamuk, non-Turkish critics defend his intertextual-based creativity: "large parts of Pamuk's aesthetics can be understood as a satire on Harold Bloom's theory of the 'anxiety of influence' (1973), with its Oedipal model of the creative imagination striving for a boundedness and autonomy of which 'originality' is taken as the sign"[46]. These kinds of similarities are common to all writers. Pamuk himself notices: "There's an English writer who goes by the name of Thomas Kyd. They say Shakespeare stole *Hamlet* from him. I've discovered another injustice too, a forgotten play by Kyd known as *The Spanish Tragedy*"[47]. In another text, he mentions that in "*The Brothers Karamazov*, Freud notes the parallels with Sophocles (*Oedipus*) and Shakespeare (*Hamlet*)"[48]. As Pamuk retells a question quoted from Tahir-ül Mevlevi (1877-1951) in *The Black Book*, imitation takes an important role in the intertextuality theory: "On the subject of personal style: the apprentice writer always begins by imitating those who come before him. This is born of necessity. Do not children also learn to speak by imitating others?"[49].

Pamuk is a postmodern author, and intertextuality is one of the significant aspects of postmodern writing that criticizes the negligence of traditions and old past culture. In Pamuk's intertextual study, he borrows old fables, pictures, and characteristics, and he narrates them in a new way. Pamuk writes about a book inside another book, and he technically changes the book to a game with the use of intertextuality. Through intertextuality, he transforms structurally hidden fictional elements of old texts into new fictions. In *My Name is Red*, painters have a fear of having their own style or being themselves. For "an author to be creative requires the purity of childhood and the fear of being punished for being creative like a child, experienced on various levels. Always the darkness of artificial unconsciousness and the satisfaction of desire await the imaginative writer somewhere in the uncanny darkness"[50]. The reason that he uses

---

[46] Halman 2010, 30
[47] Pamuk 2004, 314
[48] Pamuk 2006, 149
[49] *Ibid.*, 334
[50] Esen 2008, 29

intertextuality in his works is to make his novels more realistic by using real historical characters and events to give more force to the monotonic trajectory of the storytelling. By using historical facts, travelogues, miniatures, and other texts, Pamuk produced a new novel based on real facts.

Intertextuality shows the difference between modernism and postmodernism. The modernist has to produce something new: the modernist poet or writer expresses his subjective personal experience in an objective form and produces an original work in form and content. He must have a good knowledge of history because his work has to be unique. The postmodernist poet or writer believes there are no unique stories and combines something from a variety of texts by pastiche, parody, and collage techniques. What the modernist defines as plagiarism is for the postmodernist an original text because it is a new text excerpted from other sources. Critics of Pamuk forget that he is a postmodern author. Modern literature was born from personal issues, and it offers us a mirror to know our individuality, but postmodern literature is already on the way to delete privacy and to mutually reflect images of each mirror to others. Postmodernism offers a pleasant text by providing a kind of objectivity rather than subjectivity. Intertextuality makes it unimportant to know whether the use of a source is plagiarism or an innocent quote anymore.

Intertextuality believes that no text can be created or interpreted individually and independently from other texts. Each text is made up of sentences or words that interact with other texts. The words of a sentence are interrelated, and literary works are interrelated too. We cannot imagine the words of a sentence separated from other words. Also, we cannot imagine one literary work apart from others. Each text is an anachronistic intertext. As Jacques Derrida says: "there is nothing outside of the text"[51]; literary texts are palimpsests, meaning that the original writing has been erased and replaced with more recent writing. Sometimes intertextuality is the result of a literary genre or of discourse such as philosophy, history, science, poetry, or journalism. Laminated, nested, and newly organized texts make a new literary work. The writer uses intertextuality implicitly or explicitly through different texts. A picture, motif, or characteristic makes a theme for a postmodern writer to change and to use in a different way in his fictional work through intertextuality and mimesis. Ironically, the writer attempts to reflect real life in an alienated world. Intertextuality emphasizes that each text exists in relation to other texts, so that briefly art imitates art. Harold Bloom writes, "the meaning of a poem can only be a poem, but another poem—a poem not

---

[51] Derrida 1988, 144

itself. And not a poem [was] chosen with total arbitrariness, but any central poem by an indubitable precursor, even if the ephebe never read that poem"[52]. Thus, intertextuality is a kind of flashback.

Also, literary intertextuality borrows from a web of cultures, and as Pamuk mentioned, "we are in the company of the words of those who came before us, of other people's stories, other people's books, other people's words, the thing we call tradition," and thus it is possible for the writer to tell "other people's stories [...] as if they were his own"[53]. Pamuk "interconnects a personal dialectic with Western and Ottoman culture through intertextuality [...] by resisting an East-West dichotomy through intertextuality"[54]. In modern Turkish literature, texts that insist on the necessity of saving tradition and universal themes of Eastern and Western literature are rewritten through intertextual borrowing of textual archetypes and content. *The Black Book* examines the association of tradition-modernism or between old texts and new texts. In the background of *The Black Book*, there are quotes from the mathnavies of Şeyh Galip, Attar, and Rumi. Three texts reflect the Sufi metaphorical inner journey to reach being. In this context, Sufism is a metanarrative, Old texts as references, and *The Black Book* is the main text.

In *The White Castle*, Pamuk combines various Western and Ottoman Turkish texts and creates avant-garde trans-cultural writing in which Ottoman master and Venetian slave can enter into an intellectual discourse to understand each other's cultures. The Ottoman theme in *My Name is Red* connects a personal dialectic with Western and Ottoman culture through intertextuality. In *Istanbul*, Pamuk narrates Istanbul not only with words but also through many old family photos that create a narration of plurivocality with historical contradictions and dialectical elements. There is an intertextual play between the Ottoman archive and Republican master narratives, Sufism and secularism, and Turkish and world literature. *The New Life* is full of postmodern elements. The book is taken from other texts and is both artefact and fake, and demonstrates intertextuality in this book. Also, *The Museum of Innocence* project is rich in intertextuality: characters from other Pamuk works make frequent appearances, and the concept of the collection in the museum is everything that Pamuk has explored in the past. The book is interrelated with his memoir, *Istanbul: Memories and the City*. Even the house in *Silent House* is like a museum, filled with remnants of the past. We can extend it to his other novels, such as *Snow*. Gökberk finds similarities between

---

[52] Bloom 1997, 70
[53] Pamuk 2007, 409
[54] Huseyin 2012, 1

the protagonist, Ka and Thomas Mann's blond, blue-eyed character in *Tonio Kröger*. Before travelling to Turkey, Ka buys a charcoal grey coat from the Kaufhof in Frankfurt. The salesperson assisting him is one by the name of Hans Hansen, just like Ka uses this name, when he fabricates a story for Blue, considering that he, Ka, will be "the emissary of the Islamists and other oppressed groups in Turkey, when he returns to Germany."[55] He mentions that "Hans Hansen is the editor of a prominent newspaper, and he will publish the manifesto of the oppressed."[56]

We can discuss the originality of translated and untranslated versions of *My Name is Red*. Discussing the original text and the originality of the text is not important anymore. *My Name is Red*'s strong historical context, and the extensive relationship between art and intertextuality, make it a better novel. The consecration at the beginning of *The White Castle* shows an intertextual link with Pamuk's previous novel, *Silent House*. For readers who are familiar with that work, the saying "For Nilgün Darvınoğlu a loving sister (1961-1980)" ought to be written by Faruk, Nilgün's elder brother, in the memory of his sister who was killed in *Silent House*. Faruk is the principal narrator of *The White Castle*, and it implies that the epigraph is also Faruk's choice. Pamuk quotes chapter and verse from *Silent House*, which is thus an intertextual reference to his own literary work. Based on Brecht's alienation effect, Pamuk uses metafiction: through a variety of games he makes readers think more deeply. In this way, writers force readers to be aware that they are reading a fictional work. *The White Castle* is a good example of metafiction because it is associated with the writing of the book itself. Faruk Yücel in his critical book about *The White Castle* emphasizes that postmodern works are criticized because they do not give importance to visual quality: "that is because instead of a sophisticated story that connects the reader to a dream world, they direct readers' attention to the structure and organization of the text in very ordinary or in traditional plots without texts"[57].

In a symposium Pamuk described how impressed he was by the masterpieces of Persian literature during his stay at Columbia University in New York: "Perhaps this is where I first experienced collage techniques in a rough groping manner. They call my *Black Book* also the collage book. That is true because sometimes it seems like it is a pastiche. Indeed, this experience taught me that literary creativity includes creativity in all kinds of art brought

---

[55] Gökberk 2008, 1
[56] *Ibid.*
[57] Yücel 2013, 106

together in new ways"[58]. He describes the effectiveness of these collages in *Gizli Yüz* [*Hidden Faces*]: "The hero's hidden picture became manifest in *The Black Book*, although even in the first tale it was alive. The same is true about the meanings that infiltrated *Gizli Yüz* from *The Black Book*"[59]. *The Black Book* is another work rich in intertextual elements. There is a similarity between Galip's and Aşk's story. For example, Aşk's falling into a well, and Galip's navigating a nightclub, are the same. At the end of the stories, Galip becomes Celâl and behaves like him until he writes *The Black Book*. In the other, Şeyh Galip finds Celâl as Rumi and writes *Hüsn ü Aşk*. Galip represents Şeyh Galip and his *Hüsn ü Aşk*'s Aşk character. The search to find Hüsn in *Hüsn ü Aşk* and Rüya in *The Black Book* ends in Diyar-ı Kalp ("Heart Land") in the first, and Şehrikalp ("Heart City") in the second book. Pamuk makes many citations in *The Black Book*. In Chapter 15, a group of people tell a continuous story in a night club. This part is linked with Boccaccio's *Decameron*, written in the fourteenth century, which contains a hundred tales told by a group of people sheltering in a villa. In Chapter 17, Galip and a group of people visit Mars Model Workshop. An architect describes this workshop as "A Model of Inferno" which reminds us of Dante's *Inferno* in the *Divine Comedy*. *The Black Book* also reminds us of Marcel Proust's *Albertine Disparue*, the story of Marcel's fugitive lover Albertine, who has left suddenly without warning, leaving a short farewell letter, as Rüya did to Galip. It is an intertextual way of depicting love affairs. Also, *The Black Book* is similar to Paul Auster's narration in the *New York Trilogy*. "What makes *The Black Book* more than a set of variations on an intertextual theme—with bits of Kafka, Joyce, Calvino, Proust, and Mann joining the collage—is precisely its setting in Istanbul. The detective story is simply an excuse for Galip to wander around Istanbul, and for Pamuk to explore the byways of *hüzün*"[60]. Although Pamuk starts *The Black Book* with a quotation from Adli, who does not accept using epigraphs because they kill "the mystery" in work.[61], while shaping his work, Pamuk benefitted from Eastern culture as a valuable treasury and used various forms of tradition in his work. Postmodern elements and structures make him free to observe his world in contrast to other cultures and to search missing pieces of the cultural puzzle in his narratives. By tracing the cultural similarities and shared history, language, and literary roots, Pamuk investigates ancient Persian literature. Although the Persian language was used during the

---

[58] Aral 2007, 174
[59] Pamuk 1993, 120
[60] McLemee 2006, 1
[61] Pamuk 2006a, 3

Ottoman Empire, today it is an unfamiliar language for most Turkish people. Pamuk positively embraces old Persian literature, which has an affinity with the ancient narrated times. For example, he finds *One Thousand and One Nights* or *Kelile and Dimne* as the common ethnic and cultural heritage of both nations. Galip finds out that Celâl took his stories from the *Mathnawi* and adapted them to today's Istanbul. Pamuk himself exemplified what he had done in literature: "They call *The Black Book* a collage book. It is correct to a limited degree because sometimes it is like sticking on something together. This experience taught me that creativity bonds together something that nobody brings side by side in literature or even the other arts. After that there should be cross fertilization between them."[62]

---

[62] Aral 2007, 174-75

Chapter 11

Classical Eastern Literary Masterpieces Represent Literary Easternization

One of the major approaches of comparative studies such as comparative literature is questioning intertextuality in the territory of world literature. David Damrosch's theory of world literature attaches importance to literary masterpieces. Pamuk borrows and transforms near eastern masterpieces in his novels. Eastern comparative literature theorists, like Taha Neda, who believe in the theory of oneness between literary works of Islamic nations, admit that comparative literature must be worked on different Eastern languages such as Turkish, Farsi, and Arabic. In his non-fiction and memoirs, such as *Other Colours*, *Istanbul*, and *The Naive and the Sentimental Novelist*, Pamuk recalls his literary background: when he studied Eastern literary masterpieces and how they affected his literary comprehension. *The New Life*, *Silent House*, and *The White Castle* are full of references to Azeri and Ottoman-Turkish ports such as Fuzûlî and Nâilî. In *My Name is Red*, *The Black Book*, and *Snow*, Pamuk continually through narratives, columns, stories, and confessions relate happening stories of novels to tales of Eastern and especially Persian literary masterpieces. Aimfully or purposelessly, Pamuk utilizes Persian or Arabic classical treasures unveiled in literary masterpieces to introduce Eastern values. Presented Eastern oriented aesthetic values of Sufism in Farsi and Arabic literary works in Pamuk's novels, introduce the cultural richness of Eastern worldview to Western readers. Likewise, it is an excellent explanatory of Literary Easternization. We can categorize used masterpieces into three sections of romantic poems and didactic Sufi thematic literary works.

11.1. Masterpieces of Eastern Romantic Literature

The contribution of Eastern literature to world literature is highly underappreciated. For decades, Eastern literary masterpieces have been a source of inspiration for writers. In this spirit, Eastern masterpieces, and especially Persian literature, introduces a global republic of letters in the age of Easternization for new authors of love stories, literary works, and international perspectives. By necessity, scholars and technocrats noticed first masterpieces, such as the Arabic and Farsi works. Romantic epic poems of Persian literature, for instance, are considered as *Romeo and Juliet* in

Western literature. Furthermore, these Romantic epic masterpieces were written years before Shakespeare's dramas. In the concept of world literature, Pamuk opens new realms for his Western readers about prior romantic masterpieces. He reminds us centuries earlier when Eastern poets produced works in the same class with Western masterpieces. In *My Name is Red*, Pamuk refers to Nizami's two love stories, *Khosrow and Shirin* and *Layla and Majnun*. Nizami, known as Nizami Ganjavi, lived and died in Ganja, which is part of Azerbaijan today. Ganja was a city which at that time had mainly an Iranian population. "The direct impact of Nizami is apparent on later poets. Great poets of Farsi literature like Rumi, Sa'di, and Hafiz were not spared from this impact"[1]. Orientalist Jan Rypka, in the preface of *The Seven Beauties* by Nizami, mentions that "Some people have just heard Nezami's name, but they have not recognized his supreme position. That people of our age do not know Nezami as he deserves, does not mean he is not a valuable person, but it shows our people's incapacity to know him and his great status"[2]. Nizami is best known for his five long narrative poems, called *Quinary*. *Layla and Majnun* is the third of these five books. Ali-Shir Nava'i (1441-1501), Fużūlī and Jami were prominent poets who wrote narrative poems about this story, but none of them were as successful as Nizami.

The story of Layla and Majnun was known in Persian in the early ninth century. Other well-known Persian poets such as Baba Taher (eleventh century) and Rudaki (tenth century) had mentioned the love story earlier. The poem is based on the popular Arab lovers. There are two stories about their love affair. In one, Qeys and Leyla were from the same tribe, and they were shepherds in childhood. In another narrative, the poet Qays falls in love with his cousin Layla, but her father does not allow them to marry. Qays starts singing of his love for Layla in public. For eight years after finishing *Khosrow and Shirin*, Nizami did not or maybe did not want to, write any prominent narrative poems. In 1192, Shirvanshah ordered him to write a poem about this story. Nizami was not eager to write the poem but could not disobey the ruler, so he finished the book in about four months. There are lots of accessory materials in Nizami's book that eclipsed the main story. Mahjoub, the former professor at the universities of California and Strasbourg, believes that "In fact Nizami during the writing of these descriptions, puts "Leyli" in place of Shirin and puts the Arabian desert in the place of western Iran's attractive gardens and changed Shirin to Leyli"[3]. In *My Name is Red*, one of

---

[1] Servat 2013, 80
[2] Shahabi 1958, 12
[3] Mahjoub 2002, 94

three miniaturists suspected of the murders tells a story from history that uses a semi-illusion effect of *Leyla and Mejnun*. In this story, a king defeats another king and captures the territory and harem of the vanquished king. The conquering king orders the miniaturists to set about replacing the face of all portraits of the defeated king to himself in the manuscript pages. The defeated King had a beautiful portrait of himself as Mejnun and his "belle of beauties, his teary-eyed wife" Nariman, as Leyla[4]. The beautiful woman requests the new king, who is her new husband, to not change this portrait. The new king agrees, but a strange feeling annoys him for five years. One night he enters the library, opens a volume of *Leyla and Mejnun* and in place of the face of the previous king, he draws himself. As he was not a good artist, the librarian finds the king's archenemy's face in the place of Mejnun beside the Nariman-faced Leyla. This gossip provoked the king's soldiers and emboldened the King's archenemy. In his first attack, the ruler of the neighbouring country defeated, captured, and killed the king who imagined himself to be immortal as Mejnun. The new ruler established his own sovereignty over his enemy's library and harem and became the new husband of the eternally beautiful Neriman Sultan[5].

Khosrow and Shirin is the second of Nizami's *Quinary*, written after *The Treasury of Mysteries* and before *Leyla and Mejnun*. The story depicts the love of Sassanian Khosrow II Parviz toward his Armenian princess Shirin and ends with their marriage. Before Nizami, Ferdowsi in *The Epic of Kings* mentioned this story. It is based on a true story, but the narration is a bit different. In *The Epic of Kings* Ferdowsi emphasizes that the court was not happy about King Khosrow's love for Shirin. Before Khosrow, Shirin was a trollop. Khosrow shows a golden pad, infected blood and filth, to the priest and the court, and asks: How do you find this pad? Everyone accepts it is ugly. Khowrow orders to clean it with soil and water. When it was clean, he ordered to fill it with the musk odour filled with rosewater. Then he tells the priest that this pad was as such and became this. Nizami writes that because Ferdowsi wrote this story in his sixties, he omitted the love story and focused on the political aspects of the narrative. An artist courtier of young Khosrow praised the beauty of the Armenian ruler's niece. The artist courtier hung three pictures of Khosrow on a tree in her pathway. In *My Name is Red*, Şeküre tells how Black was affected by this scene. She tells while Black was working with her father, he had seen this picture many times and had twice made exact copies by eyeing the

---

[4] Pamuk 2001, 86
[5] *Ibid.*, 87

original and after falling in love with her, Black made a copy for himself; far and away, in place of Hüsrev and Shirin, he portrayed himself and Shekure[6].

Shirin fell in love with Khosrow's picture and escaped from the palace. In *My Name is Red*, Pamuk reminds us of the story that the picture sent with the letter which depicts pretty Shirin gazing at Hüsrev's image, falling in love[7]. In Khosrow's palace, there is a rift in the relationship between father and son. The courtiers conspired, and Khosrow fled to Armenia. Shirin was swimming in the river, and the displaced Khosrow was watching her but did not know her. Now, Khosrow falls in love with Shirin. In *My Name is Red*, the dead miniaturist finds the importance of the scene that Hüsrev was spying the naked Shirin bathing in a lake at midnight[8] more than any other details. Later, Shirin reached Khosrow's palace and stayed there. Khosrow went to Rome and married there. In another part of the story, Farhad falls in love with Shirin, but later Khosrow tortures Farhad and forces him to excavate a mountain until he dies. *Shirin and Farhad* is Vahshi Bafqi's narrative poem about Shirin and Farhad's romantic fable. It seems that Nizami defends Farhad's true love against Khosrow's unbridled lechery. In the debate between Khosrow and Farhad, Farhad notices that this universe is not for chivalrous people with modesty, but for shameless and impudent cowardly fools. Nizami tries to give moral lessons, and that is why at the end of the story, Khosrow becomes a nondiscriminatory mystic cenobite. Also, Shirin sacrifices her capriciousness to pure love.

In *The Epic of Kings*, Shirin goes to Khosrow's tent and drinks venom to die, but in *Khosrow and Shirin*, Shirin commits suicide and dies, like King Khosrow. Khosrow is killed by his son, and Shirin commits suicide over the body of her murdered husband. In *My Name is Red*, Pamuk retells the story by the murderer: "I refer to Nizami's version, not Firdusi's"[9]. One of the great scenes is when Khosrow is outside of his palace, talking with Shirin on her balcony. Black, in *My Name is Red*, compares his love story with Şeküre to the fable of *Khosrow and Shirin*: "I thought how my visit to her at the window on horseback closely resembled that moment, pictured a thousand times, in which Hüsrev visits Shirin beneath her window"[10]. In another part, Black says: "what I want to stare at for all eternity is my beloved's delicate face" because

---

[6] *Ibid.*, 47
[7] *Ibid.*, 45
[8] *Ibid.*, 27
[9] *Ibid.*, 21
[10] *Ibid.*, 41-42

the scene wherein Shirin falls in love with Hüsrev after seeing his picture reminds of "none other than her"[11].

Basically, on the one hand, stories of *Layla and Majnun* and *Khosrow and Shirin* are exceptions in Farsi literature. That is because of the presence of women as a superior character on display in the story. This point shows Nizami's giving value against women. In both of the stories, we become aware of the moral element at the sight of the two women. Shirin is more virtuous than Khosrow Parviz. In comparison with him, she is more wise and straightforward in love. Because Leyla hid love when he was burning in the fire of love, some people find her place higher than Majnun, who did not hide his love.[12]

11.2. Didactic and Sufi Thematic Eastern Masterpieces

In the concept of Easternization, studying common moral effects is a critical element. With the coming of Islam, the administrative community played a significant role in enabling the rise of the Arabic Golden Age, which later passed on the texts of the classical world and resulted in the Western Renaissance. The establishment of the Abbasid Caliphate in Baghdad (750-1517) occurred primarily because of Persian support. Armed with the power of the newly founded Islamic religion, the Persians were allowed to assume a dominant role in spreading Islamic culture mixed with morality in their literary works. The Persian scholars succeeded in changing the culture of the Caliphate from a narrow Arabic tradition into a cosmopolitan outlook of morality. Those works consist of essential masterpieces of world literature today. Sufi masterpieces, as a genre of the New Age Movement, play a critical role in Pamuk's works. Didactic poems of morality on the one hand, and Sufi stories, on the other hand, are reflected in Pamuk's works through intertextuality and play a crucial role in enabling us to demonstrate Literary Easternization theory in the realm of the Easternization thesis. Didactic works of Sa'di, the epic of Ferdowsi, and Sufi poems of Attar, Al-Ghazali, Jami, Rumi, and Shams are some of the works mentioned in Pamuk's works.

Sa'di was one of the major Persian poets and literary men famous for his social and moral thoughts in Western sources. His best-known works are poetry: *Bustan* [*The Orchard*], completed in 1257, and the verse *Gulistan* [*The Rose Garden*] in 1258. *Garden* is the best written Farsi prose ever. It consists of eight parts about kings, dervishes, contentment, taciturnity, youth for love, senescence, the impact of education, and politeness. Jami in the introduction

---

[11] *Ibid.*, 397
[12] Servat 2013, 340-41

of *Abode of Spring*, which is modelled upon the *Garden*, calls the book "not the *Garden*, but a shrine of Heaven." "Sa'di tries to escape from evil and to live only goodness and beauty"[13]. Those influenced by Sa'di include Jean de La Fontaine (1621-95), who translated his works, Daniel Defoe in *Robinson Crusoe*, Balzac in *Father Goriot*, Goethe, Voltaire, and Victor Hugo. Rypka in *The Cambridge history of Iran* writes, "Sa'di's unique and lasting success lies above all in his universally accessible and accommodating moral philosophy. The Persian, as well as any human being, can see himself in Sa'di"[14]. Pamuk in *My Name Is Red* praises Sa'di, through his murderer character under hypnosis, for the beauty of Sa'di's prose that is full of "happiness and calm" that every reader would understand "the moral" of Sa'di's story: to live in that paradise where happy mares and stallions live, "open your eyes wide and actually see this world by attending to its colours, details and irony"[15]. Pamuk narrates stories from *The Rose Garden* in *My Name is Red*. The murderer in the story is a wise person like those we confront in Sa'di's works. He tells different stories such as the story of the teacher who falls in love with his handsome student from Sa'di's "Rosegarden"[16]. In Sa'di's works "lots of elders appear in the role of advisors"[17], and Pamuk's murderer character follows the same role to retell a story from Sadi's *Garden*.[18]

Ferdowsi (935–1025) is the author of the world's longest epic poem created by a single poet, *Shahnameh* (*The Book of Kings*). *Shahnameh* is the national historical epic of Iran and the Persian-speaking world over the courses of several thousand years. *Sohrab and Rustum* by Matthew Arnold increased *Shahnameh*'s reputation. *Shahnameh* is the poetic form of *The Book of Kings of Abu Mansuri*. In his narrative poetry, Ferdowsi did not use Arabic words. "If it weren't for Ferdowsi and *Shahnameh*, maybe today a country with Iranian nationality and Farsi language might not exist"[19]. The reign of the Sassanid dynasty by small tribes was unbelievable to the Persians. The tyranny and sensuality and hedonism of Khosrow Parviz, the protagonist of *Khosrow and Shirin*, resulted in a twenty-four-year war against the peasantry and lost the people's support. His later execution was accompanied by the fall of other kings, and people lost their respect for the government. Although it was

---

[13] Zarinkoob 2010, 251
[14] Boyle 1968, 601
[15] Pamuk 2001, 342-43
[16] *Ibid.*, 95
[17] Shimizu 2011, 140
[18] Pamuk 2001, 342-43
[19] Riahi 2011, 23

difficult for Arabs to capture Iran and develop their Islamic culture, it occurred. As the right to write history lies in the hands of the conquerors, we have no idea about the first centuries of Baghdad's Arabs' probable brutality in Iran after Islam. To commemorate this great literary work, "UNESCO announced 1990 as the year of *Shahnameh*". Ibn Hisham, in the biography of the Prophet Muhammad, *Al-sīra al-Nabawiyya*, writes about the propagation of Islam by the Prophet Muhammad. An Arab Pagan, Nadr ibn al-Harith, was sitting in his place and narrating the story of Rostam and Esfandyar. Arabs believed his story is better than the Prophet's rendition[20]. Another important point about Ferdowsi's work is that "he sympathizes with all disaster victims, Iranian or Non-Iranian. He never reveals the misery of anyone, even his enemies. He never insults people and never holds grudges against anyone"[21]. After the fifth century, to feel safe Iranians started to write stories to strengthen national unity. Fear of Türkic tribes' attacks recalled the Touranian attacks (they called the Türks, Turanian). In *My Name is Red*, Pamuk reminds us of this historical truth that in the *Book of Kings*, Persian and Turanian armies clashed with all their force[22]. These are some of the reasons why Pamuk chose *The Book of Kings* in *My Name is Red*. Black's uncle in the novel says these epic scenes are beautiful works of art. The miniaturist depicts the most vital scenes to beautify the manuscript: the scene that lovers lay eyes on each other for the first time; the hero Rüstem cutting off the head of a devilish monster; Rüstem's grief when he realizes that the stranger he has killed is his son[23]. Pamuk's characters feel each scene of the story and arouse our curiosity to follow these stories. As one character narrates "I appeared in Ghazni when *Book of Kings* poet Firdusi completed the final line of a quatrain with the most intricate of rhymes" or, "I was there on the quiver of *Book of Kings* hero Rüstem when he travelled far and wide in pursuit of his missing steed"[24].

Rostam is higher than the Titans in Greek mythology or the Superman of Nietzsche; he is "a symbol of a universal perfect person who is the pride of nature"[25]. No other hero can bear the killing of his son. "In none of the great epics is there a brighter image or more enchanting role than this complete person"[26]. Except for the Simurgh, a gigantic winged creature in the shape of a

---

[20] Hashemi 2010, 42
[21] *Ibid.*, 92
[22] Pamuk 2001, 396
[23] *Ibid.*, 30
[24] *Ibid.*, 224
[25] Zarinkoob 2010, 36
[26] *Ibid.*, 37

bird, equivalent to the Western phoenix, there are no supernatural heroes, and even the demons are humanlike. *Shahnameh*'s heroic features are greater than Homer's works. The limited powers of the heroes, without introducing the power of the gods, make this book more believable. In India, "they title the wrestling champion of the country as 'Time's Rostam'"[27]. In *Snow*, Pamuk's religious character describes Rostam as "a tireless warrior of unequalled bravery who lived in Iran. Everyone who knew him loved him. They called him Rüstem, and so shall we"[28]. Pamuk describes the legendary Rüstem was a mysterious warrior who surprised everyone when on the third day of the war between Persian and Turanian armies, the Turanians sent "the wily Shengil into the field" to learn the identity of a mysterious Persian who had killed the great Turanian warrior[29].

The murderer's story in *My Name is Red*, recalls important scenes of *Shahnameh*. Pamuk gives a clue by reminding us "that the depiction of Death" was inspired by familiar scenes from *Book of Kings*—like the scene of Afrasiyab's decapitation of Siyavush, or Rüstem's murder of Suhrab without realizing this was his son[30]. When we find out that it is rivalry and bigotry that caused the crime, Pamuk recalls that the cutting of the throats of Iraj and Siyavush from behind, "arose out of sibling rivalry," in the *Book of Kings*, is always "provoked by an unjust father"[31]. "A terrible fate prevails in Rostam and Sohrab's painful story from the unyielding sense of honour and revenge. It does not have the womanlike weaknesses of the *Iliad*, which is born of love and women. That is why in *Shahnameh* power and greatness of heroes are more proverbial"[32]. When curious Turanians ask about the identity of Rostam on the day of battle between Iranians and Turanians, he answers, "My name is Death"[33]. In *My Name is Red* the murderer reminds us of crimes in various stages of history from Ferdowsi's point of view. He describes how "Satan duped Dehhak into killing his father [...] in the beginning of the *Book of Kings*" or how legendary Rüstem unknowingly killed his son Suhrab, commander of the enemy army that Rüstem had battled for three days[34]. But regret is another sense Pamuk evokes in us by reminding us of when Rüstem "beat his breast in tearful anguish" when he found the armband he had given the boy's

---

[27] Riahi 2011, 344
[28] Pamuk 2004, 78
[29] *Ibid.*
[30] *Ibid.*, 136
[31] *Ibid.*, 443
[32] Zarinkoob 2010, 42
[33] Pamuk 2001, 454
[34] *Ibid.*, 470-71

mother years ago and found the killed enemy is his own son whose chest "he'd ravished with thrusts of the sword"[35]. It is a sorrowful story when we see it in *Snow*; Pamuk narrates Rostam's son's dreams to hold justice on the world: "My father Rüstem and I will bring just rule to Iran and Turan—in other words, to the entire universe!"[36]. Pamuk's character describes both heroes as "these two great and good-hearted warriors"[37].

One Thousand and One Nights is a compilation of Middle Eastern and South Asian folk tales during the Islamic Golden Age (8th–13th centuries) in Arabic. The work was collected over many centuries and were originally folk stories of the King Shahryar and his wife, Scheherazade. Stories are in the form of a frame narrative, a story within a story mostly in prose. From the first English language edition (1706) it is known as the *Arabian Nights* in English, and the British explorer and Arabist Richard Francis Burton's translation is the most famous version of it. Some editions contain only a few hundred nights while others include more. The first European version was translated into French by Antoine Galland from an Arabic text. Galland's version of the Nights was the most popular version in Europe. It also included stories that were not in the original Arabic manuscript. Aladdin and Ali Baba's stories appear first in Galland's translation and cannot be found in any of the manuscripts. He wrote that he heard them from a Syrian Christian storyteller, Hanna Diab. King Shahryar of the Sassanid dynasty discovers that his brother's wife is unfaithful, and he starts to marry virgins and execute them the next morning before they have a chance to dishonour him. These were "slave girls," "sultan's wives," and "houris"[38] as the protagonist of Pamuk's *The Black Book* introduces them. Scheherazade, the vizier's daughter, begins to tell the king a tale but does not end it. The king, curious about the rest of the story, is forced to postpone her execution. It continues for one-thousand-and-one nights. Scheherazade later becomes the wife of the King and mother of his children. Miquel, a scholar of Arabic literature, believes "Good words own honor beyond human power... The origin of *One Thousand and One Nights* is based on the magic word and its sorcery"[39]. Some of the book's world-famous characters are Aladdin and his wonderous oil lamp, Ali Baba and his "Open Sesame" phrase to enter the forty thieves' cave, Sinbad, the Sailor, the Grand Vizier of the Ottoman Empire, Arab Abbasid caliph Harun al-Rashid and his

---

[35] *Ibid.*
[36] Pamuk 2004, 79
[37] *Ibid.*
[38] Pamuk 2006a, 42
[39] Miquel 2008, 55

vizier, Jafar al-Barmaki, and the great Arab poet, Abu Nuwas. Although the last real figures lived two centuries after the fall of the Sassanid Empire, they are part of the stories. Pamuk refers to the stories about "the fiends who invade the vizier's harems" [40] in *The Thousand and One Nights*. Alaaddin's shop in *The Black Book* figures in much of the narrative, and that is also the place where Rüya is found shot in it. Alaaddin is a real person who owns a grocery shop in Nişantaşı, Istanbul where you can find everything you need. In *The Black Book*, he is also a character in the story. Alaaddin, the owner of the shop, sells foreign literature books and it seems he affected Pamuk by the world he brought to him. He reminds Pamuk of the world of *One Thousand and One Nights* that Pamuk repeatedly studied in the summer of 1959 when he was seven-years-old. Based on Alaaddin's name, Galip describes the history of *One Thousand and One Nights* since it was first written:

I would also tell him that the tale that bore his name had not originally featured among the stories told during the famous thousand and one nights; it was a story Antoine Galland had slipped into the book when it was published in France two hundred and fifty years ago. What's more, it was not Scheherazade who had told Galland the story but a Christian woman named Hanna. I went on to explain that this woman was actually an Aleppo scholar whose full name was Yohanna Diyab, and that it was clear from the story's descriptions of coffee that the story itself was Turkish and most probably set in Istanbul.[41]

Probably the stories were translated into Arabic in the early eighth century, and Arab stories were added to it in later centuries. From the thirteenth century, more stories were added in Syria and Egypt, many of these showing a preoccupation with sex or magic. In *The Black Book*, Galip tries to find a further inner layer of stories. He discovers the historical significance of the Egyptian ban on all scenes in *The Thousand and One Nights* in which the women of the harem "made assignations with their black slaves[42]. The influence of the Sanskrit fables and Indian folklore like *Kelile and Dimne* is obvious in these stories. The important point is that stories finish happily, and morality and positive figures are victorious. "By searching different countries and collecting folk stories apart from the world of *One Thousand and One Nights* and if necessary, by referring to the memory of nations, it reveals what is the main way to address mythology, themes, and fairy tales of almost everywhere in the world"[43]. *The Black Book* is "a strange and complex

---

[40] Pamuk 2006a, 113
[41] *Ibid.*, 42
[42] *Ibid.*, 252
[43] Miquel 2008, 51-52

composition, with the second story beginning before the first was finished, and a third story beginning before the second was finished—endless stories, begun only to be discarded"[44].

Jami was the greatest Sufi poet of the 15th century. *Haft Awrang (Seven Thrones)* is his most famous poetical work, of which seven books were finished in seventeen years, until 1485. Jami completed the work on the mathnawi form. Jami was born in Khorasan, now Afghanistan. After Jami's death, the Timurid Empire's minister, Ali-Shir Nava'i, wrote *Khamsat ul-Mutahayyerin* about him. In *Seven Thrones*, Jami follows the poetic style of Nizami. Abdolhossein Zarinkoob (1923-1999), a prominent scholar of Iranian literature, believes this book practices Nizami's style in *Khosrow and Shirin* [45]. Two of the seven books in *Seven Thrones* are *Layla and Majnun* and *Joseph and Zulaikha*. Zarrinkoob believes that Jami's "*Leyla and Majnun* is not different from what Nizami and Amir Khosrow said. It is the same style, but it emphasizes more of the Arabic tales [...] Even a few methnawis have tried to ruin the complete imitation...In *Joseph and Zulaikha*, he had found another scholarly way in *Khosrow and Shirin*"[46]. *Joseph and Zulaikha* is the Quranic verse of Joseph the prophet, and Zulaikha is a military wife. Zuleikha is furious at Joseph for resisting her attempts to seduce him, and she falsely accuses him of attempted rape. The murderer in *My Name is Red* mentions the romance of *Joseph and Zuleyha* shows "envy is the prime emotion in life"[47]. In the Holy Quran, the brothers ask Jacob the Prophet to let Joseph go with them. Joseph is said to have been extremely handsome. On the way, Joseph's brothers throw him into a well. They return to their father, the Prophet Jacob, without Joseph, and the father weeps himself blind. Pamuk in *My Name is Red* narrates the same famous story by a murderer who is aware of Nizami's stories. It seems that Olive killed Elegant Effendi and threw him in a well. Later, when they find Elegant Efendi, we can compare the similarities between these two stories. "After he was removed from the bottom of the well where he'd lain for four days, his brothers scarcely knew him"[48]. The murderer reminds the Midian merchants who were pulling Joseph from the pit where he had left by his jealous brothers[49]. He reminds the romance of

---

[44] Pamuk 2006a, 113
[45] Zarinkoob 2010, 293
[46] *Ibid.*
[47] Pamuk 2001, 121
[48] *Ibid.*, 120
[49] *Ibid.*, 121

Joseph and Zuleyha, by telling that "envy is the prime emotion in life"[50]. When Bayezid II of the Ottoman Empire invited Jami, he accepted. It coincides with the time setting of Pamuk's *The White Castle*. In his way, he found out that the plague is spreading to Istanbul, and he refused to visit the Sultan but gave his work to him, and the Sultan compensated him later. The Sultan has requested him to write a comparative book based on the divine topics of Sufism. In *Luxury Durra*, Jami defended Al-Ghazali's antiphilosophy tradition that was started by Al-Ghazali's *The Incoherence of the Philosophers*. They believed in the higher importance of the Sufis' opinions of philosophers. "Turkish scholars believe that Jami's poems were of great importance in the evolution of Farsi and Ottoman Turkish poetry"[51]. Pamuk in *My Name is Red* reminds us that the "loss of faith that Jami refers to in his poetry is 'the dark night of the soul'"[52] from a character's perspective.

Al-Ghazali was a Muslim philosopher and mystic in Persian literature and one of the most influential Islamic thinkers in history, and his writings were noticed by Western scholars more than any other Muslim thinker. We can talk about the effects of "al-Ghazali in Orientalist scholarship as a remarkably self-aware, pre-modern religious thinker, propelled by an existential yet disciplined curiosity embracing fiqh (law), Kalam (theology), Falsafa (philosophy) and Tasawuf (Sufism or mysticism)"[53]. Al-Ghazali's individualism addresses the needs of the community. His doctrine is "the negotiation in his conscience between the attendant demands of individualistic commitment and communal (or contractual) participation"[54]. Pamuk refers to Al-Ghazali's works in *My Name is Red* when he refers to Islamic worldviews. A character proves his faithfulness when a heavenly angel compares his dialogue to Al-Ghazali's sense of faith: "just as Gazzali had stated in *Pearls of Magnificence*, he sweetly said: 'Open your mouth so that your soul might leave'"[55].

Kelile and Dimne is the original Sanskrit work written around the third century BCE in ancient India. It is a collection of interrelated animal fables in verse and prose. The aim of this political book is to teach landowning regulations and etiquette to Indian princes, and their manners toward subordinates. At first, it was translated into Middle Persian in 570 CE by Borzuya and then into Arabic by a Persian translator, Ibn al-Muqaffa. "From

---

[50] *Ibid.*
[51] Haravi 1998, 300
[52] *Ibid.*, 314
[53] Mitha 2001, 2
[54] Mitha 2001, 101
[55] Pamuk 2001, 213

the time *Kelile and Dimne* was translated from Arabic to Farsi by Nasr Allah Munshi in 1121 in Lahore, Pakistan in the time before Sa'di's *Garden* was written, it was known as the excellent Persian prose book. Afterwards, the *Garden* was considered and kept its place up to now"[56]. It consists of twenty parts. Some parts are Indian, and other parts are Persian stories that were later added. According to *The Book of the Kings*, Khosru I Anushiravan, the King of the Sassanid reign, sent the greatest of physicians, Borzuya, to India to find or buy the book he has heard praises about. It was translated into more than ninety-three languages. In the fifteenth century, Hossein Vaez Kashefi did a good translation. This version was translated into Ottoman Turkish, and Sultan Mustafa III gave it as a gift to Louis XVI of France. The French translation of this book made it known in the Western world. *Kelile and Dimne* is a story inside a story. A storyteller tells a story to someone, they discuss it, and one of them says if you treat it in this way, you will get the result as in the story. They agree and continue with five stories inside each other. That is the kind of storytelling Pamuk use in *My Name is Red*. According to *The Book of the Kings*, when the protagonist of *Khosrow and Shirin*, Sassanid Khosrow II Parviz, when a rebel enemy reads *Kelile and Dimne*, he is sure that he will lose the war. Also, the famous Abbasid caliph, Al-Ma'mun, wrote a summary of *Kelile and Dimne* that he kept with him every moment. In *My Name is Red*, Pamuk retells a wise story about the lack of trust in others and rational behaviour in any condition. The story is about the forced friendship between the cat and the mouse from *Kelile and Dimne* in which a poor mouse, caught between the attacks of a marten on the ground and a hawk in the air, finds his salvation in an unfortunate cat caught in a hunter's trap. Later, the cat, pretending to be the mouse's friend, licks him, thereby scaring away the marten and the hawk. In turn, the mouse cautiously frees the cat from the snare[57].

Attar, a Persian poet, was born some time previous to 1150. Like Abu Said abol-Khayr and Ghazali, he was born at Nishapur of Khurasan as centres of Sufi mysticism. His mausoleum is located in Nishapur, Iran and was built by Ali-Shir Nava'i in the sixteenth century. Attar means "perfume seller", and he was a rich business person who was selling perfumes and drugs. One day a dervish, who was far advanced in the spiritual life, came to his store and asked for a bottle of perfume with tears and deep sighs. Attar, disturbed by this unwanted visitor, tells him to pass on his way. The dervish says: "My baggage is light, for it consists only of this patched robe that I wear, but for you, with these sacks full of precious drugs, when the time comes for you to

---

[56] Mahjoub 2002, 249
[57] Pamuk 2001, 365-66

depart hence, how will you take them with you?... Attar was profoundly affected by the words of the dervish, and his biographer says that his heart became "as cold as camphor." He gave up his shop, abandoned his profession, and entirely renounced all worldly affairs"[58]. In *The Black Book*, Pamuk refers to the twelfth-century poet, Attar's self-esteem and simplicity despite his wealth, calling him, "a simple shopkeeper"[59]. Attar's *The Conference of the Birds* is a long poem about the birds that gather to decide who is to be their king. The Hoopoe, the wisest of them suggests that they should find the legendary Simurgh, a winged gigantic Phoenix bird, which means "thirty birds." The Simurgh represents immortality or God in this story. They pass a long way. As Attar in the "Hoopoe's Answer" writes, "Love needs pain and suffering. Love needs tales of bitterness." Eventually, only thirty birds remain and each of the thirty birds in the course of wandering, represent a human fault that prevents a man from attaining enlightenment. When they reach the place of the Simurgh, they find a lake where they can see their reflection. In *The Black Book*, Pamuk refers to a distich from the "Statement of Knowledge Land" part of *The Conference of the Birds*: "A hundred thousand secrets will be known when that surprising face is unveiled and shown"[60]. In another part, Pamuk introduces Attar as a Sufi "being lost in the valley of mystery"[61]. For Pamuk, the Sufi traveller finally understands that he is in "Mount Kaf" and achieves "'absolute union with God'" or the absolute[62].

Rumi (1207–1273) was a Persian poet and Sufi mystic. His poems have been widely translated into many languages, and he has been described as the most famous poet and the best-selling poet beside Omar Khayyám (1048–1131). In Iran and Turkey, he is known as Mawlānā, which means "our master." Rumi's works are written mostly in Persian, and his *Mathnawi* is one of the great literary glories of the Persian language. *Mathnawi*, one of the greatest works of mystical poetry, is a six-volume poem that teaches Sufis how to reach their goal of being in true love with God by using anecdotes and stories derived from the *Quran* and quotes from the prophet Muhammad. Until he was forty years old, Rumi was not a poet, and even after knowing Shams, he did not write poetry for a long time. Those unaware of Rumi's life, think that his *Sonnets* were written by Shams and that the *Mathnawi* was written by his student Husam al-Din Chalabi, who is praised by Rumi in the

---

[58] Smith 1932, 12-13
[59] Pamuk 2006a, 347
[60] *Ibid.*, 293
[61] *Ibid.*, 260
[62] *Ibid.*, 261

book. While writing his sixth volume of the *Mathnawi*, Rumi gave up writing the rest. "Through hundreds of languages, Rumi tries to teach tartuffes and showy people that everyone has a way to reach God"[63]. The first two volumes refer to the lower carnal self and its self-deception. The next two volumes aim to describe the benefits of reason and knowledge. The last two books argue that man must deny his physical earthly existence to understand God. *Mathnawi* starts with "Listen to this reed, how it tells a tale, complaining of separations." In *The Black Book*, the protagonist Galip tries to comprehend "the word *listen—bishnov* in Persian—which is, no less, the first word in Rumi's *Mathnawi*"[64].

What can be heard in *Mathnawi*'s straw is the story of adventurous but defeated and disabled spirit. Released of the mess and left the post of teaching and judgment. Leaving behind the storm of unique love to Shams of Tabriz, he left behind himself, and he is eager to return to his origin [...]. He is searching for a love pulling him out of the world of deception and needs and the tight world of limited physical restrictions to the unlimited original world without end. This is what Rumi hears from the straw's voice. Apart from straw, all particles in the universe have the same pricking pain and narrate the story of separation in his heart.[65]

Shams of Tabriz (1185–1248) was born in Tabriz, Iran. Before meeting Rumi in his sixties, he apparently travelled from place to place. Shams was passing by Rumi when he was reading a book. He asks Rumi about the book, but Rumi says that he does not understand the book. He throws Rumi's book into the pool of water, and its ink sprayed. Sham's lesson about the futility of school science fascinated Rumi, who was an educated Imam of Konya. He left teaching and judicial decrees and started to perform the Sema, the whirling dervish's dance, instead of praying. The disciples were displeased by their spiritual teacher's change and hated Shams and considered him to be a magician. In the introduction of Shams' *The Great Divan*, Jalal Homaei writes how after meeting Shams, Rumi said, "I was raw, I baked, and burned"[66]. In *The Black Book* Pamuk narrates the story of Rumi and Shams:

At the age of forty-five, when Rumi was, like his father before him, a sheikh in Konya, loved and admired not just by his devoted disciples but by the entire city, he fell under the influence of Shams of Tabriz, an itinerant dervish

---

[63] Mahjoub 2002, 45
[64] Pamuk 2006a, 347
[65] Zarinkoob 2010, 226-27
[66] Mahjoub 2002, 51

whose values, outlook, and learning had little in common with his own. In Celal's view, nothing about this association made any sense. The fact that scholars had been struggling to "interpret" it for seven hundred years was proof in itself. After Shams of Tabriz disappeared (or was killed), Rumi—in the face of fierce resistance from his other disciples—appointed an ignorant jeweller with no redeeming features to serve in his place. This was not, Celal insisted, proof that his new assistant induced in him the same "mystical rapture" that generations of scholars claimed he had felt in the presence of Shams of Tabriz; rather, it pointed to a man plagued by sexual and spiritual anxiety. When, after the death of this assistant, Rumi chose a third, he was every bit as dull and anodyne as the second.[67]

The Black Book is the new interpretation of the story of Shams and Rumi, with his protagonists Celâl and Galip. Pamuk quotes Rumi about "Idle men, chasing after fairy tales..."[68]. Rumi and Shams's story is a fact in Sufism, the art of rebirth. Sufism is "passing from 'I-ness' to 'he-ness' to 'one-ness'"[69]. That is why Pamuk says Celâl's death at the end of the story brings us back to Shams of Tabriz and "the corpse tossed by persons unknown into a well"[70].

Rumi's other disciples, outraged by Rumi's intimate relations with a dervish of no distinction, had made life hell for Shams and indeed threatened him with death. Whereupon Shams had disappeared from Konya on a snowy winter day—15 February 1246, to be precise. Unable to bear life without his beloved double, Rumi, who had by now received a letter informing him that Shams was in Damascus, brought his "beloved" back to Konya, whereupon he married him off to one of his daughters. But it wasn't long before the noose of jealousy began to tighten around his neck again, and on the fifth Thursday in December 1247, Shams was ambushed by a rabble, including Rumi's own son Alaaddin, and knifed to death.[71]

Galip finds something causing his confusion. "For the Arabic word for *sun* was *shams*, and Shams was Rumi's murdered lover"[72]. He looks at himself in the mirror and sighs that his love rival "read the meaning in my face ages ago!"[73]. This Self-knowledge is the beginning of a new life. "'From now on, I really am someone else!' Galip told himself, and though there was something

---

[67] Pamuk 2006a, 254
[68] *Ibid.*, 160
[69] Araste 1974, xvi
[70] Pamuk 2006a, 393
[71] *Ibid.*, 393
[72] *Ibid.*, 320
[73] *Ibid.*

childish in this thought, he knew he had embarked on a journey from which there would be no return"[74]. Although Galip accepts Shams' influence on Rumi, he asks a question about the nobility of Shams' ideas:

it was true that Rumi had fallen under Shams of Tabriz's influence the very moment he'd set eyes on him. But it was not because—as so many had claimed—Rumi had decided, after Shams had asked him his famous question and the two had plunged into their famous dialogue, that the man must be sage [...]. If Rumi were as wise as he was meant to be, he would never have been impressed by a parable so pedestrian; he would have just pretended to be impressed [...]. He had acted as if he'd seen in Shams a man of depth and powerful spirituality [...]. So the moment he set eyes on this man, he convinced himself that this was the man he'd been seeking, and of course it had not taken him much effort to convince Shams himself that he was this august person. Immediately following their meeting—23 October 1244—they retreated to a cell in the back of the *medrese*, not to emerge until six months later.[75]

Some lines show his search for a spiritual companion after Shams' death, like "How much longer do I seek you, house by house, door to door? How much longer, corner to corner, street by street?"[76]. After Shams, Rumi found another companion in Salahud-Din-e Zarkub, a goldsmith, for ten years. After his death, his favourite student, Husam al-Din Chalabi was his companion. Pamuk through his characters investigates this choice. In *The Black Book*, Celâl found "the 'sexual and mystical' intimacy"[77] of Rumi toward a man. In *The Black Book* Pamuk through his characters refers to Rumi's erotic story and asks the aim of the poet by writing such lines. Characters wonder about Rumi's aim in writing such a story when critics regarded the *Mathnawi* as the Persian-language Quran. Pamuk wonders why Rumi as the great mystic poet included the woman who died while making love to a donkey in the fifth book of his *Mathnawi* for the story or the lesson that "could be drawn from it"[78]. In this story, the housemother cites how their slave girl satisfies herself. Rumi teaches, if you are not completely aware of what you are doing, do not continue. Housemother dies because she is not familiar with what she experiences. Pamuk writes through his characters that "the story, like all stories, stood only for itself, though Rumi had also seen fit to drape it in the veil that conveyed its lesson".

---

[74] *Ibid.*
[75] Pamuk 2006a, 255
[76] *Ibid.*, 251
[77] *Ibid.*, 254
[78] *Ibid.*, 86

In *The Great Divan*, Rumi gradually liberated himself from his historical, social self. Rumi named *The Great Divan* as *Diwan-e Shams-e Tabrizi* in honour of Rumi's spiritual teacher and friend Shams. In *The Black Book*, Pamuk tells us Rumi gathered up all the poems he had written, but instead of putting his own name to them, he signed them as Shams of Tabriz[79]. Even Galip finds an article written by Celâl which starts by stating that Rumi's most celebrated work, *Mathnawi*, "from start to finish"[80] is plagiarism. Pamuk retells Rumi's story about the competition between the two famous painters[81]. Before Rumi, this story was narrated by Ghazali and Nizami. In a painting competition between Chinese and Romans, the Sultan judges which country's painters are better artists. Chinese artists painted pictures, but Roman artists just polished canvas. At the end, when the retaining curtains were removed, the shadow of pictures of the Chinese artists was reflected on the canvases of the Roman and was even better than the original pictures. Pamuk, through Rumi's *Diwan-e Shams-e Tabrizi* and through Celâl's articles and their ideas that are reflected in Galip, emphasizes, they should not worry about plagiarism, because all the secrets are hidden inside "the paltry books" they have read and write, and all the world's secrets are hidden inside "the mirror of mysticism."[82] Then, he reminds Rumi's story, "The contest between the Two Painters"? which is borrowed from "someone else, from himself"[83].

---

[79] *Ibid.*, 261
[80] *Ibid.*, 258
[81] *Ibid.*, 361
[82] *Ibid.*, 91
[83] *Ibid.*

Chapter 12

Logoteunison: The Social Theory of Easternization Behind Literature

Literary Easternization is the Easternization of the Western mind through literature. Literary Easternization is an evidence-based reasoning system that uses inductive reasoning in the premises and supplies strong evidence to prove the truth of the conclusion. Although the truth of the conclusion of an inductive argument is probable and also based on evidence, it is a logical argument that makes a generalized fact more comprehensible by the use of instances. Although inductive reasoning is inherently uncertain and allows for the possibility that the conclusion is false since it is based on the truth of the premise, it is more comprehensible reasoning based on common sense.

Let's exemplify. Most Iranian women memoirists received a Western-style education and had received international literary prizes and became bestsellers, generally in the United States or Britain. Satareh Farman Farmaian, Nahid Rachlin, Azar Nafisi, and Firoozeh Dumas' memoirs are some of these bestseller books. An autobiography becomes a bestseller when written by a celebrity, but memoirs can be written by common people, and all of these memoirists were not famous at the time of writing their memoirs. Afghanistan-born Khaled Hosseini published three novels, all of which were bestsellers, and two of them were on *The New York Times* Best Seller list for more than a hundred weeks. Based on the *Evening Standard*'s report on 8 October 2015, Orhan Pamuk's *A Strangeness in My Mind* was London's bestseller fiction. Japanese Haruki Murakami is another million-copy bestseller. You can find Kazuo Ishiguro's novels in any European or American bookshop. Pakistan-oriented Hanif Kureishi, or even Egyptian Naguib Mahfouz, and Nuruddin Farah from Somalia are other examples of Successful Eastern writers in the West. Considering a bestselling authors' stance brings about this question: What lies behind Eastern-oriented stories that are interesting for Westerners?

I think world literature prepares a substructure for world-wide literary works to share their world view together. Natively, describing Literary Easternization is possible by use of the Easternization thesis. Easternization is a crystallization of Eastern worldviews in the Western mind, mixing them to make a global worldview. Easternization puts cultures and their subcategories under psychiatric observation. Literature needs to be observed as a social and communicative system that reflects the broader cultural horizon. Already comparative literature is used by literary critics to study cultural elements inside fictions and especially non-fiction literary works. Consequently, Literary Easternization reflects the Easternization thesis in world literature. It is a reflection of an Eastern worldview crystalized in literary works that are accepted by the Western mind. Does Easternization aim at anything beyond showing similarities of Eastern and Western minds? Literary Easternization in the context of world literature aims to show why Western readers prefer Eastern values. I call Literary Easternization, "Logoteunison."

Logote (λογοτε) is a Greek word that means "literary." It represents the literary background of Western culture stemming from the Greeks. In addition, "Unison" means coincidence in pitch of two or more musical voices or tones, which end as a perfect prime. A tuneable performed piece needs an accord of all chords. I think world literature, regardless of the nationality that produced it, produces a pleasant song, similar to a perfect symphony. Without considering running time of any musical instrument, each one plays a role in a symphony's unison. A nation's literary work adds new values to world literature and is open to expert investigation. So, *Logoteunison* reminds an eager reader in Britain that if you are reading this literary work and fantasize—as did Western readers from the time of the Western publication of *One Thousand and One Nights* in the eighteenth century—that mysterious society in India, another reader in India reads Shakespeare's *King Lear*. *Logoteunison* reminds us the while Orhan Pamuk's *A Strangeness in My Mind* is a bestseller in London, E.L. James' *Grey* is a bestseller in Istanbul.

After Tanzimat reforms, during the whole previous century, the majority of novels in Turkey were about identity crises as a result of changing during the period of modified secular Turkey. After political didactic and moralistic literary movement of the modern period, postmodern literature developed a point of view toward old cults. The way Pamuk describes identity is not through differentiating and taking a stand of "us" and "the Other" but through hybridity. The identity debate in Pamuk's works is an open-ended and inconsequential argument without any conclusion. In the process of dramatizing, Pamuk tries to blur the distinction between fact and fiction by broadening differences in order to demonstrate alikeness. It brings about a strangeness in our mind when we confront characters who represent both East and West. In a paradoxical alteration due to a change of place, characters wrap themselves up in new identities. In Pamuk's *The Black Book* and *My Name is Red*, there are lots of examples that characters are transformed into new characters, with new identities. In *The White Castle*, the main characters are even transported from the Eastern part of the World to Western countries, where they are reborn, or from the Western part of the World to Eastern countries.

As mentioned, Literary Easternization relates back to an exchange of ideas, cultural values, and traditions from a consensus: Literary Easternization is a partnership in the literary field. Literature is not perceived separately from culture. Fantasy plays a significant role in American literature. We have to admit there is an excellent request for fantastic themes in literary and artistic works, but also Americans are fed up with reading fantasy novels, imagining aliens, and picturing UFOs. NASA's recons are in this direction. Americans search for signs of life on other planets, yet they do not know people from other continents.

Powerful clubs are not necessarily the winners of a soccer match. Maybe a team of good quality is a contender, but it does not mean that the team that cannot score a goal is absolutely the losing party. All competitions need men of high attainments and skills. If we accept a competition between East and West, we can liken them to clubs, with matches between teams taking place on two levels: The coaches specify the strategy, and the players carry out the strategy. The first match is in the West's field. In the previous match, held on the East's field, the West scored, and the result was Westernization. Now, in the West's stadium, the East team is outmanoeuvring. The simplest way to describe the Easternization process is to liken Eurocentric versus the East in a competition. Orhan Pamuk parallels this unidentified situation to rival brothers in a family. In *Istanbul*, he talks about the rivalry between him and his brother Şevket, which causes "anger and jealousy" that would make them forget they are brothers[1]. We can compare this rivalry from a different viewpoint as between the members of any group. If the personnel in any group assumes a major task, does it mean the other members are idle, or their tasks are unimportant? Group work needs members, and their exchange of views brings success. They win together and lose equally. Hereupon world literature is the winner, and high and low are equal participants in this crowded contingent. Huntington's *Clash of Civilizations* is changed to Khatami's theory of "Dialogue among Civilizations" or Todorov's "dialogue between civilizations"[2].

Though materialism is prevalent in society, the widespread passing of self-help books from hand to hand and their sales revenue shows that people attach importance to physical dimensions as much as spiritual dimensions. New Age spirituality or mind-body-spirit is regarded in Western society. Eastern literary works and masterpieces are inherently suffused with spirituality. Moral elements are a sophisticated content of Turkish, Indian, or Japanese works.

---

[1] Pamuk 2006b, 16
[2] Todorov 2010, 105

Humans become more individuated day by day and are distinguished from the interests of the community. Values of capitalism are exposed to criticism, yet the values of Marxism have supposedly declined. The spread of spirituality is a probable outcome. Traditional beliefs in God are changed to new concepts of supernatural energy sources. Plain and simple, Eastern mystic elements in old masterpieces offer a new worldview to the West.

The Easternization thesis through the Weberian rationalization process says that there is no way to go for the West except through the East. The Timurid dynasty or Alexander the Great was not the only conquerors in history. The Europeans discovered America and extended their territory to another continent. By weakening Native American tribes, Europeans conquered new continents. Triumph over the natives of Australia was part of the same inclination to possess more soil. After the whole new continents were discovered and pacified, there were no new places to be discovered. Former United States president, George W. Bush's project of occupying Afghanistan, Iraq, and unfinished projects of winning Iran and Syria were part of the American soul of conquest. Now it is time to discover new soil in other planets, and NASA is part of this project. Still, it is a longitudinal research project, and up to this time, the West decided to conquer the whole planet. I think if the East could compete economically and technologically, it would follow suit. The world is round, and the West found out there are specifics in the East that they missed.

An Iranian international bestseller memoirist, Azar Nafisi, remembers a few decades ago, Americans were continuously asking her, "How many camels do your parents own?"[3] in their home in Iran. At the time of new spatial conquests, Americans had no idea about the lives of other people on planet Earth. Infiltration of bigotry in the educational systems of Asian, European, and American countries and rigid viewpoints, assign different meanings to East and West. The most critical task of art and literature is to eliminate distances between poles and assign a different meaning to them. Film festivals that are not subservient to the capitalist system, like the Cannes film festival, and literary honours like the Nobel Prize in literature, should undertake the duty of lightening the mood.

İstanbul and the Bosphorus Bridge join Asia and Europe, linking East and West, and also play a vital role in this sense. They act as a metaphor to show a connection between the poles. In *Istanbul*, Orhan Pamuk unveiled the mystery of rival characters in his novels. From childhood, he and his brother

---

[3] Nafisi 2008, 95

Şevket competed with each other. In consequence of rivalry between these brothers, now Orhan Pamuk is a worldwide award-winning author, and Şevket Pamuk is a well-known professor in history. From a different viewpoint, Pamuk reminds us that he lived on both the European side of İstanbul (Şişli, Beyoğlu) and the Anatolian side of İstanbul (Kadıköy). He lived in Turkey (the East) and also in the United States (the West). In *Snow*, the protagonist, Ka, lives in İstanbul, moves to the Eastern part of Turkey (Kars), and then to a European city (Frankfurt). Orhan and Ka are similar characters, whether in East or West. Pamuk was born on the Anatolian side of İstanbul, grew up on the European side, again lived on the Anatolian side, and now lives on the European side, on both sides of the Bosphorus Bridge that joins Europe and Asia. Pamuk, İstanbul, and the Bosphorus Bridge are clues to adopt the theory of Literary Easternization.

In Pamuk's *The Black Book*, the characters Galip and Celâl take over each other's positions. Pamuk's characters implicitly emulate two great Sufis: Rumi and Shams of Tabriz. Even in *The White Castle*, Ottoman Hoja and the Italian exchange roles. The overtone in these novels is that it is not wrong to exchange roles. Even when one becomes more successful, the other one is pleased with his new situation. This situation brings about a question in my mind: When Şevket got his doctorate in the United States, Orhan Pamuk could not finish his bachelor degree. Now which one looks more successful? Which part of İstanbul is better than the other side?

Hüzün, which Pamuk talks about in *Istanbul*, is not the sadness about the lost glory of the Ottoman dynasty, but the pain of losing a society that nevertheless was the capital of Islam. The Ottoman Empire included different cultures. It was a great city without clashes between Muslims, Christians, and Jews. Now, Orhan Pamuk is not dear to any political mind in Turkey because of his analysis of Turkish society, religion, nationalism, secularism, and their roles in defining identities. Contemporary Turkish society is dividable into four groups: the first group, the majority of contemporary society, believe that they are Muslims first and foremost and grieve secretly for the wane of the Ottoman Empire. Second, are the nationalists who also think of themselves as believers. Third, are the secular Kemalists, and the last group consists of minorities and socialists. Except for the last group of minorities, the other groups are not interested to hear what Orhan Pamuk has to say because of his assertions to a Swiss newspaper about genocide during the Ottoman period before the Nobel Prize ceremony, and also his criticizing of secularists and nationalists. Pamuk's *hüzün* at for the failure to create a more democratic society that does not impose its will on its citizens. At bottom, the age of Literary Easternization is the period of democracy in world literature.

Pamuk emphasizes that we need to leave nationalism and defend minority rights. He defends a kind of "internationalization" in the process of increasing involvement of enterprises, this time not in the economy, but in literature. He accepts that he is a Western-style author. His novels can be studied through postmodern concepts, and he uses magic realism in some of his novels. He uses techniques to show a mystic society with an Oriental spirit for Western readers. During the age of communication, critics expect him to show Turkey as a bed of thornless roses. That is why the majority of visitors to his Museum of Innocence in İstanbul are foreigners, not Turks. Is it possible to hide the history of a country during the Literary Easternization age of world literature? For many years Germany and France stymied Turkey from joining the EU. Now in 2015, Germany announces that they want to take a million Syrian refugees. It shows that struggles to keep Turkey out of Europe were useless at the time when more than five million Türks are living in European countries, with three millions of them settled in Germany. In globalized cosmopolitan Western societies with mixed ethnicity, turning the clock back is impossible anymore. Goethe, centuries ago, predicted "the epoch of world literature" and "everyone must strive to hasten its approach"[4].

Most bestselling writers from Eastern countries in Europe and the United States have grown up or were born in Western countries. Language plays a significant role in introducing their works to a large mass market reading community. Literary works written in the English language are in great request. David Damrosch in Chapter 7 of *What Is World Literature?* clarifies that entering world literature means being read by speakers of the same language. Also, it is linked to translation. Damrosch distinguishes world literature from "a national 'global literature'"[5] and says "work on world literature should be acknowledged as different in kind from work within a national tradition, just as the works themselves manifest differently abroad than at home"[6]. It shows that a literary work in the context of world literature can be surveyable as part of commonly used languages. Goethe, through translation, learned about Farsi literature. His devotion to Eastern and especially Persian literature was because of reading translated works. For instance, translation has a significant effect on putting Pamuk's works on the map. Usually, translators of his books are praised—as Erdağ Göknar received the International IMPAC Dublin Literary Award in 2003 for translating *My*

---

[4] Damrosch 2003, 1
[5] *Ibid.*, 25
[6] *Ibid.*, 286

Name is Red—because of their translations, and some Turkish readers find his translated books in English better than the Turkish original.

Even Edward Said confesses that his *Orientalism* is unable to answer all questions related to it nowadays as he says Orientalism is a considerable dimension of modern political-intellectual culture, and as such has less to do with the Orient than it does with 'our' world[7]. There should not be any rules in the humanities which are based on interpretations. Literary Easternization, abbreviated as *Logoteunison*, is based on evidence more than theory. As Campbell calls Easternization a "thesis," Literary Easternization is another "thesis" that is supported by hundreds and hundreds of examples. If someone has left Japan decades ago and now returns to that society, he feels it is a different country. It is common in Western societies that show slow changes. Modernization occurs in countries in different periods, but it happens sooner or later. Apart from dogmatic viewpoints like Eurocentric views or rigid religious views that are induced by politicians under the rubric of "Westernization" or "Islamic Terrorism," people are able to understand each other. At the time of the hostage crisis at the American Embassy in 1979 in Iran, there was a peak of immigration from Iran to the United States.

Postmodern literature is adaptable to new ideas. Literary Easternization is comprehensible through world literature. World literature includes old masterpieces and recently published works, and Literary Easternization is part of a postmodern literary movement that involves new and old literary works. Although there are some shortcomings in postmodernism, which cannot solve its problems and always has to quote from Nietzsche, who passed away long before the 1960s and never experienced the postmodern age, Literary Easternization is definable through postmodernism. Postmodern references to Nietzsche's ideas show that we need the past as well as the present. If not, *The Rubaiyat of Omar Khayyam* should not be a bestseller in the United States. Also, intertextuality plays a significant role in literary masterpieces in newly published literary works, as Orhan Pamuk did in his *My Name is Red* and *The Black Book*. Parody, pastiche, and mimesis play a significant role in consequence of interchanging literary masterpieces in the realm of world literature.

Literary Easternization does not rule out the relationship between history and literature. It includes the whole history of the world in the realm of "East" and "West" categories. It says that every nation has a story to tell and each one's story is worth hearing. It hears colonization stories as much as decolonization stories. Literary Easternization asks, Do we need to regard East

---

[7] Said 2003a, 12

and West as historical enemies or can we see the relationship as literary and cultural commerce? In trade, both sides can reap a profit, even if one side comes out ahead. Westerners can accept Eastern values in their lives as Easterners have accepted Western viewpoint so far. Does declaring war between cultures from a Eurocentric view or from the point of view of Orientalism make sense? These are academic topics, but they relate to life experience.

Literary Easternization and Easternization, in general, try to prove the possibility of forming a new politics of truth based on evidence. It does not try to change anyone's mind or to correct any ideology or worldview. Weber believed that results in the humanities are probable, not absolute, and Pamuk says "Nothing is pure"[8]. In his lecture to the Swedish Academy of the Nobel Prize, Pamuk stated that he hoped one day his novels "will be read and understood, because people all the world over resemble one another"[9]. He finds this desire a kind of "troubled optimism," because of his being "scarred by the anger of being consigned to the margins, of being left outside"[10]. He confessed how he followed the "love and hate that Dostoyevsky felt toward the West all his life" just "to behold the other world he has built on the other side"[11].

Seyhan asserts that the Swedish Academy praised Pamuk to "expand the purview of the novel through his intimacy with Western and Eastern cultures," and he did so by taking "the novel from Westerners" and transforming it into "something never seen before"[12]. In *The New Life*, Osman recognizes that cultures always borrow and steal and the only important matter is how we understand them. Like Talât Halman, who notes "the 'bridge' metaphor used frequently in relation to the East-West question"[13], Pamuk asserts that "My books are a testimony to the fact that East and West are coming together. Whether in peace or anarchy—they are coming together. There needn't be a clash between East and West, between Islam and Europe. That's what my work stands for"[14]. He also mentioned that "I want to be a bridge in the sense that a bridge doesn't belong to any continent, doesn't belong to any civilization, and a bridge has the unique opportunity to see both civilizations and be outside of it. That's a good, wonderful privilege"[15]. In

---

[8] Pamuk 2001, 194
[9] Pamuk 2007, 413
[10] *Ibid.*, 413
[11] *Ibid.*, 413
[12] Seyhan 2006, 1
[13] Halman 2010, 58
[14] Pamuk 2006d, 1
[15] Pamuk 2002, 1

The White Castle, it is evident at the end of the story that the Venetian felt happy in the East, and Hoja was more successful in the West.

Benedict Anderson in *Imagined Communities* clarified that the study of literature everywhere in the world is under a national concept. From the view of Easternization, no nationality is more important than any other: the books produced by the continents with the least literary wealth are as crucial as countries with the most literary wealth. While countries may strive to make themselves known for their literary wealth, Pascale Casanova thinks that such rivalries created world literature. It is a well-known fact that there was an inequality in the world of letters, where minor languages and literatures always struggled against dominant counterparts. Imagine that the History of the World extends from East to West. If Asia is the beginning, Europe is the end of History, but if the world is round, Asia and America are side by side and East meets West. Huntington stated, "The narrowing of the identities, however, has been paralleled by broadening of identity as people increasingly interact with other people of very different cultures and civilizations and at the same time are able through modern means of communication to identify with people geographically distant but with similar language, religion, or culture"[16].

Pamuk says good stories affect us profoundly and become our own stories. That is why old stories that no one knows who told them first, appeared to be original and "with each new telling, we hear the story as if for the first time"[17]. He says, "A great painter does not content himself by affecting us with his masterpieces; ultimately, he succeeds in changing the landscape of our minds"[18].

Defining literary Easternization is possible through decontextualization, which considers a matter in isolation from its context, but because literary Easternization considers the Easternization process as part of a literary survey, we have to transcend barriers of contextualization. Contextualizing provides information about the situation in which something happens in order to understand it better, which helps us to comprehend cultural studies. "Contextualizing literature in the expanded fields of discourse, culture, ideology, race, and gender are so different from the old models of literary study according to authors, nations, periods, and genres that the term 'literature' may no longer adequately describe our object of study"[19]. Thus,

---

[16] Huntington 2004, 13-14
[17] Pamuk 2007, 283
[18] Pamuk 2001, 195
[19] Bernheimer 1995, 72

Bryan Turner uses Jean Baudrillard's claim that the Gulf War was merely a television event and criticizes Edward Said's reliance on the text by telling that in the notion of textualism, Said's approach to history is problematic because there can be "no distinction between fictional writing and social reality" and an exclusionary "focus on 'textual practices' has negated the social dimension of language and meaning, and confused the materiality of social relations with an alleged materiality of the context."[20]

As dialogue is established on understanding two different subjects, Pamuk tries to invalidate and dramatize the dual discourse of East and West to achieve his purpose. He tries to explain that identifying ego is not possible without 'others.' It means that to know yourself you need to know others who are different from you, and consequently to know someone different, you should put yourself in his shoes. Switching identities is an effective way to understand multiculturalism, which shows there are no pure identities. Todorov asserts, "Dialogue, which ensures that all interlocutors have an equivalent position, is a more civilized form of communication than the harangue, in which you utter certainties while everyone else just listens"[21]. To be effective, dialogue should be a twofold requirement, "it must recognize the difference of voices engaged in the exchange, and must not presuppose that one of them constitutes the norm while the other can be explained as a deviation, or as backward, or as evidence of bad will."[22] He says, questioning our own certainties and self-evident beliefs, we should "adopt provisionally the standpoint of the other"[23].

Edward Said's "Travelling Theory" announces how theories go on in life and how they can be misused and abused. Said defined four stages for how ideas or theories travel: first, at the point of origin, we consider circumstances through which the idea was born. Second, the pressure of other contexts influences new theories as they take new shapes. Third, these stages are a set of conditions which then resist ideas or theories. The last stage is a fully or partially accommodated and incorporated idea, which means the transformation of an idea based on its new use in a new time and place. Travelling Theory points out that a theory can be misread or misunderstood by a reader almost all the time, especially as time goes on. As a result, a text or theory is always fluid, and a misreading by one person may inspire another theory. The mobility of ideas to the rest of the world can be reflected in any author's

---

[20] Turner 1994, 7
[21] Todorov 2010, 23
[22] *Ibid.*, 196
[23] *Ibid.*

opinions. Said asserts that "a theory in one historical period and national culture becomes altogether different for another period or situation"[24]. Said's Travelling Theory criticizes his own nationalistic mentality of East and West opposition. In an article Said himself explains that his defences of Islam and the Arab world in *Orientalism* is different from the view of Orientalists who show Orientalism as evil[25].

Pamuk tries to change misunderstood Orientalist views toward his Western-style novels. Expectations of love and happiness in Pamuk's works are not local, but universal identity pains. The questions of Pamuk's novels are not esoteric but overarching topics beyond Eastern or Western issues. Thereby, neither East nor West win in a diegetic, sloppy, dipole power struggle. Pamuk creates an aesthetically overrated struggle between East and West, and then he invalidates it by undermining the controversy with fabulous illustrations.

From an Orientalist view, our identity is exotic. If we look more exotic, our identity will become more defined through exchanges of East and West. Institutionalized dialogue of Orientalism in the West expects the East to provide a place on the exotic artistic level, as is shown in movie festivals, museums, art galleries, journals, and news. If Easterners are not exotic enough in any field to be seen adequately, they do not appear logical. Through Foucauldian discourse analysis, Easterners are Easterners because they are Exotic. Thus, festivals, museums, art galleries, journals, and news produce discourses, and Easterners reproduce them. Now, Orientalism as Oriental-ism is based on the East's metanarrative of the East or Islam. In this metanarrative, the Eastern is exotic because it must be different and because it must be the Other. Insisting on being exotic makes the Other more exciting and attractive for a Westerner. Exoticism helps Eastern writers to write best sellers in Western countries. In the process, they try to be seen, and intertextuality creates new opportunities. Intertextuality accommodates a multiplicity of cultural discourses and articulates an exotic "otherness."

Postmodern theorists think that when cultural studies enter comparative literature, it changes into the cultural theory that discusses the nation rather than a defined cultural formation. Postmodernists usually follow Lyotard's theories in *The Postmodern Condition*, which say that postmodern society is the end of metanarratives. Derrida's Différance throws the idea of the origin of original meaning and captures heterogeneous features in the production of textual meaning. Différance indicates that opposites are related to each other

---

[24] Said 1983, 226
[25] Said 1995, 4

integrally and there is never a moment when the meaning is complete. Différance aims to tell that there is no fact, essence, or correct, but there are lots of facts for an author. Derrida thinks whole meanings and interpretations of the text are undecidable because text can have innumerable interpretations and meanings. As Samuel Weber mentions, if criticism does not consist of "the conflictual structure of its own discursive operations," it just "reproduce[s] the constraints it is seeking to displace"[26]. Like any humanities branch, literature attempts to understand human experience in a particular style apart from philosophy, sociology, or history.

Pamuk quotes a sentence of Tâhir'ül Mevlevî, who finds writers' imitation as a necessity and asks, "Do not children also learn to speak by imitation of others?"[27]. Mimesis as imitation has been theorized by thinkers as diverse as Plato, Aristotle, Erich Auerbach, Derrida, Bhabha, and many others. The concept of Imitation or Mimesis has a historical background. Plato in the *Republic* asserts that art is imitation, which is bad. He thinks it takes the human away from the reality of self. Aristotle in the *Poetics* says art is imitation, and that's all right and even a good experience that all people within society need to acquire. Mimesis for Auerbach means that literature is an imitation of contemporary society from which it was produced. For Lyotard, the movement of the artwork toward truth is through the movement of mimesis. Michel Foucault asks "how and to what extent it might be possible to think differently, instead of legitimating what is already known? There is always something ludicrous in philosophical discourse when it tries, from the outside, to dictate to others, to tell them where their truth is and how to find it"[28]. Pamuk says it is not possible to understand how much of his utterance is "8" and how much "copied from other examples"[29]. Nor do I know how many of those examples are themselves copies of another original or copy. The same can be said of my own words. Perhaps this is why it may be best just to repeat what someone else has already said"[30].

Although, translation is a significant weapon in international literary competitions. Casanova emphasizes this universalization, Parisianization, or cosmopolitanism that is a transnational relation in the context of the other experiencing the same and denying difference, which helps us to perceive universal works. Translation acts as a device to enter the Republic of letters

---

[26] Veeser 2010, 23
[27] Pamuk 2006a, 334
[28] Foucault 1990, 9
[29] Pamuk 2007, 287
[30] *Ibid.*, 287

without the ethnocentrism of the universal governing authorities, and it proclaims the equality of all the citizens of the republic of letters[31].

I think one reason that makes world literature important is the pain everyone in the East or the West share. The age of Literary Easternization provides a chance to anyone in the East or in the West to share their experiences. Vargas Llosa reminds us of Bertolt Brecht's alienation effect, which makes the novel look faker. He says, "a [...] bad novel without charming structure cannot convince us about the rightness of arrayed lies"[32]. Brecht believed that to reach your aim in theatre plays, you need to make audiences aware of the autistic nature of plays. Llosa thinks the novel should act the reverse of plays to convince readers about the truth of events in the story. I think Vargas Llosa's struggle to be realistic is an important fact in the era of Literary Easternization, and it affects Westerners' responses to Easterner's pains, beliefs, and way of life. Pamuk says, "the novelist strives to express his own personal worldview while also seeing the world through the eyes of others"[33].

Barthes in the "Death of the Author" asserts that the birth of a reader results in the death of the author, and it means that in a new place and different time, the text finds a new meaning that the author did not intend. Death of the Author means a new interpretation in which language speaks, not the author. Also, a text is a context full of quotes from different cultural centres which are definable through intertextuality. Pamuk works both Western and Eastern elements equally in a parody form to show their differences as much as their similarities. Using irony, Pamuk moves away from identity problems when he talks about it. Pamuk denies being dependent upon identities since he explores identity problems through parody. Fredric Jameson argues that parody, which is an allusive imitation of another cultural production, is replaced by pastiche, which is a kind of collage and mechanism of intertextuality that celebrates the work it imitates. Jameson defines pastiche as a new term for "the imitation of a peculiar or unique, idiosyncratic style, the wearing of a linguistic mask, speech in a dead language"[34]. He explains, "But it is a neutral practice of such mimicry, without any of parody's ulterior motives, amputated of the satiric impulse, devoid of laughter and of any conviction that alongside the abnormal tongue you have momentarily borrowed, some healthy linguistic normality still exists. Pastiche is thus blank

---

[31] Casanova 2004, 133-37
[32] Vargas Llosa 2004, 45
[33] Pamuk 2011b, 144
[34] Jameson 1991, 17

parody, a statue with blind eyeballs"[35]. Pamuk references Chinese, Indian, and Persian stories that are full of allegories that are reflected in *The Black Book* like a Dadaist collage setting in contemporary Istanbul. He sets mentioned Eastern origin rewritten stories in an American style detective plot. He says the reason to write such a story is that he could not write "a social commentary about Turkey's problems" and he had to try something else.[36]

Pamuk by use of intertextuality combines Western works and Ottoman period works. The revival of a hybrid history of East and West in Pamuk's personal experience of Istanbul made him a modern national literary writer in a new way by interpreting old masterpieces. Huseyin writes, "Pamuk's use of conflicting themes has undoubtedly forced him to reconsider the Turkish modern. But it goes without saying that perhaps Pamuk cannot consider himself as a Turkish modern unless East and West are synthesised and embraced, if not experienced, by resisting an East-West dichotomy through intertextuality"[37].

---

[35] *Ibid.*, 17
[36] Pamuk 2007, 367
[37] Huseyin 2012, 1

Conclusion

In this book, I have described how cultural Easternization in the West, influenced by Eastern worldviews, has created a change in readers' approaches to world literature. Instead of the statistical study of the sales of Eastern-oriented novel writers' in the West, or analyzing which topics are the most popular topics by Western readers about Eastern cultures, I have instead demonstrated that Orhan Pamuk is an example par excellence of Easternization theory, and the theory of Literary Easternization. The popularity of Pamuk's works—which reflect Eastern values being adopted by Western readers—is also a clear example of a rising global interest in little-known cultures for readers from different cultures. My theory of *logoteunison* reveals a mixing of Western worldviews with Eastern worldviews with the most telling examples, such abounding examples of unanalyzed literary works detracts us from understanding this orientation period correctly. For example, novels with "harem" in their titles are in demand for Western readers. Such an exotic title for Western readers guarantees good sales rate in Western countries, but such facts are misleading. However, demonstrating the main functions of Easternization in a literary work through literary theory makes any term easier to support. Thus, intertextuality, as one of the dominant theories in literature, is a good tool to indicate the adaptations of Western and Eastern worldviews in Pamuk's works. In 2008, Sociologist Colin Campbell defined Easternization as influencing "beliefs and values" of people living in European countries or the United States, because of the penetration of "Eastern forms of thought"[1]. Campbell's *Easternization of the West: A Thematic Account of Cultural Change in the Modern Era* is the only book pursuant to cultural effects of Easternization in the humanities. Easternization can be described briefly:

[1] The Easternization thesis is impossible to describe apart from Max Weber's theory of culture. Weber defined subcultures based on certain values or worldviews. Worldviews are important because they give us a sense of the world and also help us to understand a global concept of culture. Weber accepted the world as a meaningful cosmos. He believed in rationalization and neutrality in social research. He defined ideal (pure) types to show that the social sciences are abstract and uncertain. As a neo-Weberian, Campbell defined Easternization based on Weber's ideas. Social scientists before Weber were studying human life

---

[1] Campbell 2008, VIII

in society objectively. Weber tried to understand the meaning of social behaviour through concepts such as sympathy or empathy through interpretive realization, which means that reality should be considered through self-study, not from a researcher's perspective. Weber's idea can be extended to Pamuk's works, which reflect Campbell's Easternization thesis. Pamuk chose Istanbul a city between East and West, to show Western and Eastern lifestyles without interpreting any of them. His novels are an uncritical reflection of social facts in a country between Western Europe and Eastern Asia. Westernized Pamuk, whose avatars are imbued with Eastern literature, political events in Turkey, religious discrimination, and cultural diversity, prefers to remain neutral about contradictory topics in his country. For example, in *The Museum of Innocence* and *A Strangeness in My Mind*, he talks about sex before marriage and the perspective of Westernized and conservative families toward it.

[2] Easternization or "East in the West"[2] is based on people's behaviour and beliefs or, briefly, their worldviews. It is a compilation of "Eastern worldviews" that "exist within the civilization of the West"[3]. Easternization for Campbell is not the process of de-Westernization but the impression of the East upon Western culture without any domination. It should not be identified as the colonization of the West: Rather, it can be a way to confront renewed Western values and worldviews. Campbell thinks that secular, rationalist and scientific worldviews have appeared in the East because there was no other choice. He thinks the birthplace of Eastern beliefs and values are not essentially Asian but are ideal worldviews for *both* Eastern and Western cultures. *Consequently, we can summarize Easternization as cultural adaptation and assimilation of Eastern worldviews in the civilizations of the West, or the choosing of Eastern values in the cultures of the West.* Pamuk gives the example of two clocks to emphasize this adaptation. He says that when they show the same hour, it does not mean that one is imitating the other clock. If they show different times, we cannot say that one is right and another is wrong. He says, "To say that one is five hours ahead of the other is also nonsense; by using the same logic you could just as easily say that it's [five] hours behind"[4].

[3] Easternization is based on Weber's "cosmos" theory, which defines the world as a "completely connected and self-contained cosmos"[5]. Easternization describes the historical meeting point of East and West, which suggests an ultimate conclusion in single world culture. Thus, Easternization points toward

---

[2] *Ibid.*, 15
[3] *Ibid.*, 39
[4] Pamuk 2006a, 153-54
[5] Campbell 2008, 58

a "one world" theory of elective indigenous cultures. Pamuk's works make this concept clear to us. Pamuk's writing career is a testament to the fact that East and West can meet rather than clash. In *The White Castle*, an Easterner and a Western scientist meet in Istanbul, a city between two worlds, and their identity change from one to the other by the end of the story. Most of Pamuk's stories take place in Istanbul, which is geographically located between Western Europe and Eastern Asia, and from a social perspective, historically naturalizes *both* Eastern and Western cultures.

[4] Although Easternization is not the process of de-Westernization or decline of the West, it is a revival of post-Western culture. For Campbell, globalization has the same meaning as Westernization because cultural globalization is under the effect of Western values or movements happening in the West. Although Campbell does not mention it in his book, Easternization is different from any possible cosmopolitan society as defined by Kwame Anthony Appiah, because cosmopolitan society is an imaginative community based on equality of economic, political, and even moral rights, but Easternization is based on evidence, not imaginative theories. Also, I believe the concept of Easternization cannot be studied through the concept of multiculturalism, which includes the acceptance or existence of multiple different cultural traditions. Easternization is not a matter of respecting cultural diversity of ethnic or religious groups, but an overt result of eagerness through available evidence, and understanding the logic of that evidence.

[5] Easternization posits that the scientific mind could not answer Westerners' questions about the universe. Campbell reminds us that widespread propagation of New Age Movements fills the gaps left behind by the lapse of myth and superstition. New Age Eastern-style worldviews fill the gap left between modern science and the waning of organized religion. Fundamentally, Campbell believes the popularity of Karma, reincarnation, Zen Buddhism, Krishna consciousness, yoga, meditation, t'ai chi, and fang shui show the importance and the attraction of traditional Eastern worldviews, but he also accepts that Easterners need to care more about their saleable products because there is much of value in Western culture, which also is in search of new alternatives. After all, Easternization observes classical concepts of Christian theology mixed with a range of Eastern perspectives, from dualistic materialism to metaphysical monism. The most popular traditional Eastern worldview is Sufism, which is optimized in Pamuk's works. We can say that Pamuk gets the most out of Sufism to attract the Western mind that is interested in Eastern worldviews. Put more clearly, I do not know any other well-known contemporary novelist who reflects any Eastern-oriented worldviews better than Pamuk's use of Sufism in the literary works.

[6] Easternization is the reverse of Edward Said's *Orientalism*. Easternization does not inspect the historical process of the interaction between the East and the West, but takes a neutral view toward the East-West divide: *Orientalism* studies ancient civilizations of Arab-Islamic heritage, while Easternization aims to interpret the present based on evidence and fact. It disallows rumours that insist Muslims cannot understand Christianity or on the contrary, the Christians cannot comprehend Islam. Rather, Easternization explores the realities of the contemporary present to address the question of "Who are we?" in a time of post-Orientalism, post-Occidentalism, and Easternization. Even Edward Said confesses, Orientalism is a considerable dimension of modern political-intellectual culture.[6] By selecting Istanbul as the setting place of his novels, Pamuk specifically emphasizes that he takes a neutral view toward the East-West cultural distribution. In his early novels such as *The Black Book*, *The New Life*, *Cevdet Bey and His Sons*, *Snow*, and even *The Museum of Innocence*, his protagonists are settlers of wealthy neighbourhoods of Istanbul, and in his latest novel, *An Strangeness in My Mind*, for example, the novel's protagonist is a 'Slumdog' of Istanbul, but all of his characters take a neutral view toward each other. Generally, Pamuk's protagonists change their living place from the European side of Istanbul to the Anatolian regions of Turkey, and vice versa.

[7] Although Campbell accepts that the probable causes for the expansion of Eastern values in the West after World War II are because of postmodernization and the "decline of modernity"[7], there are differences between postmodern worldviews and the Easternization thesis. While postmodernization captures the period after modernity, the Easternization period includes a period of post-Christianity. While postmodernism cannot clarify the mechanism of transformation of modern culture to postmodern society, the Easternization thesis, through the West's characteristic rationalization, suggests the process of "the rise of the East in the West"[8]. Campbell asks, How is postmodernism, which is against grand-narratives, going to explain the new trends of New Age-style Eastern grand-narratives? Perhaps it demonstrates an inner conflict within postmodernism. Huntington believes, that "the world is becoming more modern and less Western"[9].

Studying the Easternization process of literary works can be discussed via Literary Easternization. Literary Easternization investigates the Easternization

---

[6] Said 2003a, 12
[7] Campbell 2008, 360
[8] *Ibid.*, 362
[9] Huntington 1996, 78

of the Western mind in literary reading. Like Easternization, Literary Easternization is an inductive reasoning system supported by evidence. Literary Easternization can be described through a few rules:

[1] As Easternization is defined through a "cosmos" theory, Literary Easternization as a concept of world literature tries to show how Western readers prefer Eastern values merged in literary works. I call Literary Easternization "Logoteunison," which consists of "*logote*" and "unison." *Logote*, with Greek and Latin roots, underlies the literary and theoretical background of Western literature. Logoteunison means the literary rapport of all world literatures. Literary Easternization, based on the evidence, proves that other nations' literary works are interesting for others. Logoteunison says everyone has a story to tell and everyone's story is worth hearing. Hence world literature plays a key role in the comprehension of Literary Easternization. Nearly two centuries ago, Goethe stated that "National literature is now a rather unmeaning term; the epoch of world literature is at hand, and everyone must strive to hasten its approach"[10]. David Damrosch indicates that world literature is an approach to literature whereby reading literature makes our worldview. Damrosch says, "world literature is always as much about the host culture's values and needs as it is about a work's source culture"[11]. He thinks these dealings create a "double refraction" in which both the host and the source cultures provide "the two foci that generate the elliptical space within which a work lives as world literature [connecting] both cultures, circumscribed by neither alone"[12]. Damrosch, the head professor of Columbia University, played a great role during the writing process of *The Naïve and the Sentimental Novelist* by Pamuk, who was a lecturer Columbia at the time. Pamuk's ideas about the novel are similar to Damrosch's views about world literature. Damrosch views world literature as more about the "host culture's values and needs," than the "source culture." The view is ideally reflected in Pamuk's works, who is an international best-seller author who writes about the East-West conjunction symbolized by the city of Istanbul, known for its betweenness of two cultures.

[2] The widespread appearance of self-help books in Western countries shows us that people attach importance to physical dimensions as much as spiritual dimensions. As Easternization emphasizes, New Age spirituality of mind-body-spirit has been catching on in Western societies, along with Eastern literary works or masterpieces. Traditional theism changes to new concepts of supernatural sources and New Age Movements. Eastern mystic

---

[10] Damrosch 2003, 1
[11] *Ibid.*, 283
[12] *ibid.*

elements in old Eastern masterpieces offer a new worldview to the West. Pamuk's oft-told stories about Sufis like Hallaj, Shams, and Rumi, and mystic stories of old-time literary masterpieces, is a conscious cultural presentation of Eastern worldviews for Western readers who show interest to supernatural sources and New Age Movements. *My Name is Red* and *The Black Book* are two great paragons of their genre since they articulate Eastern worldviews to be investigated by Western readers. Chapter 3 is an intertextual study of these elements in Pamuk's novels.

[3] Easternization through the Weberian rationalization process states that there is no way to go for the West except toward the East. New space research is in order to discover mysterious new lands in the universe. This inclination is to process more soil, and Westerners realized there are parts in the world not completely discovered or explored. Easterners found out there are non-negligible specifics in the East that they have missed. That is why there are Iranian female memoirists, and Afghani and Japanese authors' books that are international bestsellers on the shelves of booksellers in Western countries. It shows that there are Eastern-oriented stories that are interesting for Westerners. Perhaps Pamuk utilizes intertextuality to find a place for himself in the Western book markets. Using Eastern literary masterpieces provides an opportunity for Pamuk to show the literary and cultural richness of the East in a roundabout way to the Western reader who is eager to find new meaning in his life.

[4] Most bestseller Eastern-oriented writers in the United States or Europe have grown up in Western countries. They usually use English fluently, and it helps them to reach readers in greater numbers. It is obvious that books written in popular languages or translated works into those languages help them to muster more support through global readers in the territory of world literature. Through translation, Goethe reached Farsi masterpieces, and now through translation, scholars can become aware of precious international literary works. Erdağ Göknar and Maureen Freely won prizes for their translations of Pamuk's works. They contributed to the success of Pamuk's works. Damrosch's *World Literature* states that translated literary works make source culture more valuable. The manner of representing Eastern values through Eastern masterpieces for Western readers was made possible through the translation of Pamuk's works, which optimized good examples of world literary works.

[5] There is an intimate interaction between Literary Easternization, postmodernism, and world literature. Although Easternization criticizes postmodernization for its inner conflicts, describing Easternization as a literary process without using postmodernist terms seems absurd. Easternization relates to a "cosmos," and Literary Easternization, through postmodern thinkers' theories, is open to all thoughts and ideas. The interaction between products of the world through intertextuality, pastiche,

Conclusion

and collage plays a great role in familiarization for readers of world literature, whether with old masterpieces or unnoted literary works. Denial of history is not compatible with Logoteunison. The whole history of world literature is worth hearing about. Colonization or decolonization stories outside of Eurocentric or any dogmatic viewpoint are worth hearing about, and the Western mind sympathizes with protagonists of world literature novel as much as any reader in any Eastern country. Bestselling Eastern works prove Literary Easternization's assertion.

The presentation of a new concept in literary study that is not obvious requires explanation and examples to remove doubts of a theory or thesis. Orhan Pamuk is a well-selected author to remove doubt in defining Literary Easternization for several reasons:

[1] In the concept of world literature, he is a well-known novelist whose books have been translated into more than sixty languages. He won the prestigious Nobel Prize in literature, which provides an opportunity for every reader of world literature to follow Easternization materials in his works.

[2] Critics accept that Pamuk is a Western-style writer, which is a reason that critics compare Pamuk with Paul Auster, Umberto Eco, and other postmodern authors who use magic realism in their works.

[3] Pamuk refers to Persian, Arabic, Sanskrit, and Ottoman Turkish masterpieces through intertextuality, which helps the reader of Western world literature to gain sufficient knowledge about great Eastern literary works.

[4] Sufism, which is a source of the New Age Movement, plays a crucial role in most of Pamuk's works. His reference to great Sufis and their lives in his stories are sufficient evidence of the connectedness between his works and Easternization's persistence in Western minds eager for New Age worldviews. Showing interest in Sufism, Pamuk justifies why Sufism is alluring to Western minds.

[5] In his non-fiction Pamuk shows he is in competition with his brother, which is reflected in his works such as *The White Castle*, *The Black Book*, and *My Name is Red*.

[6] "East" and "West" as terms can be studied as rivals, but instead of believing in Huntington's "Clash of Civilizations," Pamuk suggests a "Dialogue among Civilizations." İstanbul and the Bosphorus Bridge, which links Asia and Europe and also binds East and West together, show a connection between poles. The European and Anatolian sides of İstanbul, separately, act as a metaphor to demonstrate this connection between East and West. Sometimes this connection is shown in Pamuk's novel as protagonists who change their positions and adopt new roles.

[7] The *Hüzün* of İstanbul is another theme based on Lyotard's *Tristesse*, which is a sadness of losing sight of the soul of the Ottoman period, including different ethnicities and cultural diversity.

Although some thinkers believe that consequential losses of Western objectivism and Eastern spiritualism, may have destroyed the possibility of compromise between East and West, Easternization, on the contrary, illustrates that Western culture gives consequence to Eastern worldviews. Literary Easternization or as I call it, Logoteunison, says that the general theory of comparative literature, or Damrosch's "world literature," coordinates Eastern and Western worldviews to further the understanding of worldwide prominent literary masterpieces. My proof of this claim is Western readers' interest in Eastern-oriented literary author's works. By taking into consideration contemporary bestseller Eastern-oriented writers such as Pamuk, we meet on a common ground of Eastern-oriented literary masterpieces. The most important feature of these masterpieces is the lore of Eastern mysticism. Orhan Pamuk as a well-known author influenced by Western authors, including their mode of thought and lifestyle, and he also grew up in Turkey with access to an Eastern cultural background, which provided a good opportunity to reveal cultural features of both East and West. However, the Easternization thesis underlines the impact of Eastern worldview manifested in Westerners' perspective. As world literature that captures belletristic on an extended period of time, Literary Easternization gathers up literary works from past to present as part of world literature and offers global readers literary treasures from the East and the West. In this way, comparative studies such as comparative literature or world literature enact interactive relations among literary works and cultures. The universal language of independent spirit revealed in Pamuk's works as Sufism and other Easternoriented writers such as Eastern mysticism as the clearestcut examples of human experience integrated into literature. Therefore, distinguishing differences between Eastern and Western literary works in an age of cosmopolitanism appears to be a sterile discussion. In developing a putative clash between East and West, we should primarily specify *which* East or West we are discussing. The "West," for example, is reviewable in the context of geography (Europe and the Americas), culture (United States, Britain, Germany, France, etc.), religion (Christian, Jewish, new philosophical schools), industry (United States, Germany, etc.), military (NATO), colonialism (France, Britain, etc.), liberalism (Greece), secularism (Turkey), and so on. Clearly, it is possible to specify different categories when defining the East. It is evident that non-attributive interactive relations cause misunderstanding. Therefore, dogmatic Eurocentric or Orientalist enlighteners are rejected nowadays. The most important feature of Easternizaton is that it is not *against* Westernization. In order to avoid misunderstanding, I note over and over again that Easternization is opposed to and against *Orientalism*. Easternization does not aim to query Orientalism or examine Eurocentrism in detail but strives to distinguish itself from them. Adopting understanding and interaction instead of rejection, hostility, and confrontation should be Easternization's field of study. The full approval or negation of the West is not useful for the East so that moderate, positive, and impartial scientific, cultural, political, and economic relations is possible through objective perspectives toward Western culture and civilization. Easternization emphasizes reciprocity and positive cognition of the East in the West, and Literary Easternization speaks to intertwined works of world literature manifested in *Logoteunison* and the alignment of literary works grounded in their cultural contents and sites.

References

Abrams, M.H. *A Glossary of Literary Terms*. Fort Worth: Harcourt Brace Jovanovich College, 1993. Print.

Afridi, Mehnaz Mona and David M. Buyze. *Global Perspectives on Orhan Pamuk: Existentialism and Politics*. New York: Palgrave Macmillan, 2012. Print.

Anderson, Benedict. *Imagined Communities: Reflections on the Origin and Spread of Nationalism*. London: Verso, 1991. Print.

Appiah, Kwame Anthony. *Cosmopolitanism: Ethics in a World of Strangers*. New York: W.W. Norton & Co., 2006. Print.

———. *The Ethics of Identity*. Princeton, NJ: Princeton University Press, 2007. Print.

Aral, Fahri. *Orhan Pamuk Edebiyatı: Sempozyum Tutanakları*. İstanbul: Sabancı Üniversitesi, 2007. Print.

Arasteh, A. Reza, and Erich Fromm. *Rumi the Persian: The Sufi*. London: Routledge and Kegan Paul, 1974. Print.

Arendt, Hannah. *The Origins of Totalitarianism*. Orlando, FL: Harcourt, Brace, 1973. Print. Harvest Book.

Bakhtin, Mikhail. *Problems of Dostoevsky's Poetics*. Trans. Caryl Emerson. Minneapolis: University of Minnesota Press, 1984. Print.

———. *The Dialogic Imagination: Four Essays*. Ed. Michael Holquist. Austin: University of Texas, 1981. Print.

Barthes, Roland. *Image, Music, Text*. Trans. Stephen Heath. London: Fontana, 1977. Print.

———. *The Pleasure of the Text*. Trans. Richard Miller. New York: Hill and Wang, 1975. Print.

———. *Writing Degree Zero and Elements of Semiology*. London: J. Cape, 1984. Print.

Bernheimer, Charles, ed. *Comparative Literature in the Age of Multiculturalism*. Baltimore, MD: Johns Hopkins University Press, 1995. Print. Re-visions of Culture and Society.

Bhabha, Homi K. *Nation and Narration*. London: Routledge, 1990. Print.

———. *The Location of Culture*. New York: Routledge, 1994. Print.

Bloom, Harold. *A Map of Misreading*. New York: Oxford UP, 1975. Print.

———. *The Anxiety of Influence: A Theory of Poetry*. Second edition. New York: Oxford University Press, 1997. Print

Boyle, John Andrew. *The Cambridge History of Iran*. Vol. 5. Cambridge: Cambridge University Press, 1968. Print.

Campbell, Colin. *The Easternization of the West: A Thematic Account of Cultural Change in the Modern Era*. Boulder, CO: Paradigm Publishers, 2007. Print.

Carrier, James G. *Occidentalism: Images of the West*. Oxford: Oxford University Press, 2003. Print.
Casanova, Pascale. *The World Republic of Letters*. Trans. M.B. DeBevoise. Cambridge, MA: Harvard University Press, 2004. Print.
Césaire, Aimé. *Discourse on Colonialism*. Trans. J. Pinkham. "Introduction," R.Kelly NewYork: Monthly Review Press, 2000. Print.
Clayton, Jay, and Eric Rothstein, eds. *Influence and Intertextuality in Literary History*. Madison, WI: University of Wisconsin Press, 1991. Print.
Dabashi, Hamid. *Post-orientalism: Knowledge and Power in Time of Terror*. New Brunswick, NJ: Transaction, 2009. Print.
Dallmayr, Fred R. *Beyond Orientalism: Essays on Cross-cultural Encounter*. Albany: State University of New York Press, 1996. Print.
Damrosch, David. *What Is World Literature?* Princeton, NJ: Princeton University Press, 2003. Print.
Dawson, Andrew. "East Is East, Except When It's West: The Easternization Thesis and the Western Habitus." *Journal of Religion & Society* 8 (2006): n.p. Web. 15 Nov. 2015. <http://moses.creighton.edu/jrs/toc/2006.html>.
De Certeau, Michel. *Heterologies Discourse on the Other*. Trans. B. Massumi, Minneapolis, MN: University of Minnesota Press, 2000. Print.
Derrida, Jacques. *Limited Inc*. Evanston, IL: Northwestern University Press, 1988. Print.
———. *The Other Heading: Reflections on Today's Europe*. Bloomington, IN: Indiana University Press, 1992. Print. Studies in Continental Thought.
Edib, Halide. *Conflict of East and West in Turkey*. Delhi: Jamia Millia, 1935. Print.
Ellwood, Robert S. *Religious and Spiritual Groups in Modern America*. Englewood Cliffs, NJ: Prentice-Hall, 1973. Print.
Esen, Nüket, and Engin Kılıç . *Orhan Pamuk'un Edebi Dünyası*. İstanbul: İletişim Yayıncılık A.Ş., 2008. Print.
Fanon, Frantz. *The Wretched of the Earth*. Trans. Richard Philcox. New York: Grove, 2004. Print.
———. *Black Skin, White Masks*. New York: Grove Weidenfeld, 1967. Print.
Foucault, Michel. *The History of Sexuality: The Use of Pleasure*. Vol. 2. Trans. R.Hurley New York: Vintage, 1990. Print.
Fox, Richard Gabriel, ed. *Recapturing Anthropology: Working in the Present*. Santa Fe, NM: School of American Research, 1991. Print.
Freud, Sigmund. *The Complete Psychological Works of Sigmund Freud*. Ed. James Strachey. 1st ed., Vol. 14. New York: W.W. Norton, 1976. Print.
Gokalp, Ziya. *Turkish Nationalism and Western Civilization: Selected Essays of Ziya Gökalp*. Trans. Niyazi Berkes. New York: Columbia University Press, 1959. Print.
Gökberk, Ülker. "Beyond Secularism: Orhan Pamuk's *Snow* and the Contestation of 'Turkish Identity' in the Borderland." *Konturen* 1 (2008): n.p. Web. 15 October 2015. <http://journals.oregondigital.org/konturen/article/view/1286/1326>.

Guillén, Claudio. *The Challenge of Comparative Literature*. Trans. Cola Franzen. Cambridge, MA: Harvard University Press, 1993. Print.

Haravi, Najib Mayel. *Jam-i*. Vol. 45. Tehran: Ṭarh-e No, 1998. Print. Iran and Islamic Culture.

Hashemi, Seyed Mohsen. *Shahnameh Ferdowsi: Peykaviha Va Pasokhhaye Mohtamel [Ferdowsi's Shahnameh: Following the Analysis and Possible Responses]*. Tehran: Niloofar, 2010. Print.

Huntington, Samuel P. *The Clash of Civilizations and the Remaking of World Order*. New York: Simon & Schuster, 1996. Print.

——. *Who Are We?: The Challenges to America's National Identity*. New York: Simon & Schuster, 2004. Print.

Huseyin, Şefik. "Radical Critique: Orhan Pamuk's 'Turkish Modern': Intertextuality as Resistance to the East-West Dichotomy." *IJRC*, Vol.1, No.2 (2012): n.p. *Radical Critique*. Web. 15 November 2015. <http://www.radicalcritique.org/2012/12/Vol01No2Huseyin.html>.

Jameson, Fredric. *Postmodernism, or, the Cultural Logic of Late Capitalism*. Durham, NC: Duke University Press. 1991. Print.

Jung, C.G. *Ravanshenasi Va Shargh [Psychology and the East]*. Trans. L. Sadaghiani. Tehran: Diba, 2010. Print.

Kristeva, Julia. *Desire in Language: A Semiotic Approach to Literature and Art*. New York: Columbia University Press, 1980. Print.

Lacan, Jacques. *The Seminar of Jacques Lacan: The Ego in Freud's Theory and in the Technique of Psychoanalysis, 1954-1955*. Ed. Jacques Alain Miller. Vol. 2. Trans. S. Tomaselli. New York: W.W. Norton, 1991. Print.

Lavery, Brian. "In the Thick of Change Where Continents Meet." *The New York Times* (26 August 2003). Web. 15 November 2015. <http://www.nytimes.com/2003/08/27/books/in-the-thick-of-change-where-continents-meet.html>.

Lewis, Bernard. *What Went Wrong? Western Impact and Middle Eastern Response*. London: Phoenix, 2002. Print.

——. *Tarife Pasamodern Baraye Bacheha [Postmodern Explained: Correspondence 1982-1985]*. Trans. Azin Hossein-Zadeh. Tehran: Sales, 2005. Print.

——. *The Postmodern Condition: A Report on Knowledge*. Trans. Geoffrey Bennington and Brian Massumi. "Introduction" by Fredric Jameson. Minneapolis: University of Minnesota Press, 1984. Print.

Macfie, Alexander L. *Orientalism: A Reader*. New York: New York University Press, 2000. Print.

MacKenzie, John M. *Orientalism: History, Theory, and the Arts*. Manchester: Manchester University Press, 1995. Print.

Mahjoub, Mohammad Jafar. *Khakestar-e Hasti [Ashes of Existence]*. Tehran: Morvarid, 2002. Print.

Manguel, Alberto. "My City of Ruins." *The Washington Post* (26 June 2005). Web. 15 November 2015. <http://www.washingtonpost.com/wp-dyn/content/article/2005/06/23/AR2005062301620.html>.

McLemee, Scott. "*The Black Book.*" N.p., 23 July 2006. Web. 15 October 2015. <http://www.mclemee.com/id181.html>.

Miquel, Andre, and Jamal-Eddin Bencheikh. *Mogaddameh Bar Hezar-o Yekshab [Les Mile Et Une Nuite]*. Trans. Jalal Sattari. Tehran: Nashr-e Markaz, 2008. Print.

Miłosz, Czesław. The Captive Mind. New York: Knopf, 1953. Print.

Mitha, Farouk. *Al-Ghazālī and the Ismailis: A Debate on Reason and Authority in Medieval Islam*. London: I.B. Tauris in Association with the Institute of Ismaili Studies, 2001. Print.

Motlagh, Bahman Namvar. "Bakhtin, Dialogism and Polyphony: The Study of Bakhtine's Intertextuality." *Human Sciences* 57 (2008a): 1-18. Web.

——. *Daramad-i Bar Beynamatniyat [An Introduction to Intertextuality]*. Vol. 1. Tehran: Sokhan, 2012. Print. Literary-Artifical Theories and Critics.

——. Bakhtine, *Transtexual Study. Human Sciences* 56 (2008b): 127-142. Web.

Morson, Gary Saul. "Socialist Realism and Literary Theory." *The Journal of Aesthetics and Art Criticism*, Vol. 38, No. 2 (1979), 121-33. Web. 6 November 2015.

Nafisi, Azar. *Things I've Been Silent About: Memories of a Prodigal Daughter*. New York: Random House Trade Paperbacks, 2010. Print.

Nasr, Seyyed Hossein. and Ramin Jahanbegloo. *In Search of the Sacred: A Conversation with Seyyed Hossein Nasr on His Life and Thought*. Intro, T. Moore. Santa Barbara, CA: Praeger, 2010. Print.

Neda, Taha. *Al-adab Al-Mogaren [Comparative Literature]*. Trans. Hadi Nazari Monazzam. Tehran: Nashr-e Ney, 2004. Print.

O'Donnell, Patrick, and Robert Con Davis. *Intertextuality and Contemporary American Fiction*. Baltimore, MD: Johns Hopkins University Press, 1989. Print.

Orhan Pamuk. NobelPrize.org. Nobel Media AB 2019. Sat. 16 Feb 2019. <https://www.nobelprize.org/prizes/literature/2006/press-release/>

Orr, Mary. *Intertextuality: Debates and Contexts*. Cambridge, UK: Polity, 2003. Print.

Pamuk, Orhan. *The Black Book*. Trans. Maureen Freely. London: Faber, 2006a. Print.

——. *Cevdet Bey Ve Oğulları*. İstanbul: Iletişim, 2003. Print.

——. *Istanbul: Memories and the City*. Trans. Maureen Freely. New York: Vintage International, 2006b. Print.

——. "Orhan Pamuk: Bridging Two Worlds." Interview by Elizabeth Farnsworth. PBS, 20 November 2002. Web. 15 November 2015. <http://www.pbs.org/newshour/bb/entertainment-july-dec02-pamuk_11-20/>.

——. "The Fading Dream of Europe." *The New York Review of Books*. Trans. Maureen Freely. N.p., (10 February 2011a). Web. 16 November 2015. <http://www.nybooks.com/blogs/nyrblog/2010/dec/25/fading-dream-europe/>.

Pamuk——. *My Name Is Red*. Trans. Erdağ M. Goknar. London: Faber and Faber, 2001. Print.

———. *The Naive and the Sentimental Novelist.* Trans. Nazım Dikbaş. New York: Vintage, 2011b. Print.

———. *The New Life: A Novel.* Trans. Güneli Gün. New York: Vintage, 1998. Print.

———. *Other Colours: Writings on Life, Art, Books and Cities.* Trans. Maureen Freely. London: Faber, 2007. Print.

———. *Silent House.* Trans. Robert P. Finn. New York: Alfred A. Knopf, 2012b. Print.

———. "Struggling with the Elements of a Complicated History." Interview by Jörg Lau. *En.qantara.de.* N.p., 12 Oct. 2006d. Web. 28 Sept. 2015. <https://en.qantara.de/content/interview-orhan-pamuk-struggling-with-the-elements-of-a-complicated-history>. Previously it was published in Germany's weekly die Zeit in 2005.

———. *The White Castle.* Trans. Victoria Holbrook. London: Faber, 2009. Print.

———. "Yoksul Doğu ülkelerinde Sevilen Bir Yazarım." Interview by Cem Erciyes. *Radikal* [Istanbul] (3 September 2010c): n.p. Web. 28 September 2010. <http://www.radikal.com.tr/kitap/yoksul-dogu-ulkelerinde-sevilen-bir-yazarim-1016773/>.

Pantham, Thomas. "Some Dimensions of the Universality of Philosophical Hermeneutics: A Conversation with Hans-Georg Gadamer." *Journal of Indian Council of Philosophical Research* 9 (1992): 132. Print.

Plottel, Jeanine Parisier, and Hanna Kurz Charney, eds. *Intertextuality: New Perspectives in Criticism.* New York: New York Literary Forum, 1978. Print.

Riahi, Muhammad Amīn. *Firdausi.* Tehran: Tarh-e No, 2011. Print. Iran and Islamic Culture.

Riffaterre, Michael. "Interpretation and Undecidability." *New Literary History*, Vol. 12, No. 2 (1981), 227-42. Web.

Robinson, Dave. *Nietzsche and Postmodernism.* Cambridge, UK: Icon, 1999. Print.

Said, Edward W. *Beginnings: Intention and Method.* New York: Columbia University Press, 1985. Print.

———. *Covering Islam: How the Media and the Experts Determine How We See the Rest of the World.* London: Vintage, 1997. Print.

———. *Culture and Imperialism.* New York: Knopf, 1993. Print.

———. "East Isn't East: The Impending End of the Age of Orientalism." *Times Literary Supplement* (3 February 1995): 4. Print.

———. *Orientalism.* London: Penguin, 2003a. Print.

———. "Orientalism, 25 Years Later: Worldly Humanism v. the Empire-Builders." *www.counterpunch.org.* N.p., (4 August 2003b). Web. 14 November 2015. <http://www.counterpunch.org/2003/08/05/orientalism/>.

———. *The World, the Text, and the Critic.* Cambridge, MA: Harvard University Press, 1983. Print.

Saussy, Haun. *Comparative Literature in an Age of Globalization.* Baltimore, MD: The John Hopkins University Press, 2006. Print.

Sencer, Orhan. "Almanya Cumhurbaşkanı'ndan Orhan Pamuk'a Doğum Günü Tebriği." *Haberler*, Hurriyet.com.tr, 5 June 2017, www.hurriyet.com.tr/almanya-cumhurbaskanindan-orhan-pamuka-dogum-40480048.

Servat, Mansour. *Ganjine-ye Hekmat Dar Asar-e Nezami [Treasures of Wisdom in Nezami's Works]*. Tehran: Elmi, 2013. Print.

Seyhan, Azade. "Seeing through the Snow." *Masress. Al-Ahram Weekly* (19 October 2006). Web. 15 November 2015. <http://www.masress.com/en/ahramweekly/12033>.

——. *Tales of Crossed Destinies: The Modern Turkish Novel in a Comparative Context*. New York: Modern Language Association of America, 2008. Print.

Shaffer, Robert. "What to Teach about Asia: Howard Wilson and the Committee on Asiatic Studies in the 1940s." *The History Teacher*, Vol. 35, No. 1 (2001), 9-26. Web. 6 November 2015.

Shahabi, Ali Akbar. *Nezami, Poet and Raconteur*. Tehran: Avesina, 1958. Print.

Shimizu, Naomi. *Meyarhye Akhlaghi Dar Didgah-e Sa'di [Ethical Standards in Sa'di's Perspective]*. Tehran: Elmi & Farhanghi, 2011. Print.

Smith, Margaret. *Attar: The Persian Mystic*. New York: E.P. Dutton, 1932. Print.

Spengler, Oswald. *The Decline of the West: Form and Actuality*. 6th ed. Trans. C.F. Atkinson. New York: Alfred A. Knopf Inc., 1927. Print.

Spengler. "The Fallen Bridge over the Bosporus." *Asia Times Online*. (31 October 2006), n.p. Web. 6 May 2014. <http://www.atimes.com/atimes/Middle_East/HJ31Ak02.html>.

Todorov, Tzvetan. *The Fear of Barbarians: Beyond the Clash of Civilizations*. Chicago: University of Chicago Press, 2010. Print.

Turner, Bryan S. *Orientalism, Postmodernism, and Globalism*. London: Routledge, 1994. Print.

Vargas Llosa, M. Mario. *Cartes A Un Joven Novelista [Letters to a Young Author]*. Trans. Ramin Molaei. Tehran: Morvarid, 2004.

Veeser, H. Aram. *Edward Said: The Charisma of Criticism*. New York: Routledge, 2010. Print.

Venn, Couze. *Occidentalism: Modernity and Subjectivity*. London: Sage Publications, 2000. Print.

Weber, Max. *The Sociology of Religion*. Boston: Beacon, 1993. Print.

Yücel, Faruk. *Ötekinin Gözünden Orhan Pamuk: Beyaz Kale'yi Çevirmek*. Istanbul: Aylak Adam Kültür Sanat Yayıncılık, 2013. Print.

Zarinkoob, Abdulhossein. *Ba Karevan-e Holleh [With the Apparel Caravan]*. Tehran: Elmi, 2010. Print.

Secondary Sources

Acar, Adnan. *Nobel, Orhan Pamuk ve Yazarlığı*. Istanbul: Doruk, 2013. Print.

Adnani, Manouchehr. *Avaye Eshgh [Love Sounds]*. Tehran: Sales, 2000. Print.

Akbayır, Sıddık. *Orhan Pamuk-Yaşar Kemal: Zamansız Bir Karşılaşma*. İstanbul: Ferfir Yayınları, 2011. Print.

Akcay, Ahmet Sait. *Okumanın Farkı Orhan Pamuk: Okumanın İmkânsız Alegorileri*. İstanbul: Pozitif Yayınları, 2011. Print.

Al-i Ahmad, Jalal. *Gharbzadeghi [Occidentosis: A Plague from the West*. Tehran: Ferdows, 2007. Print.

Allen, Graham. *Intertextuality*. London: Routledge, 2000. Print.

Almond, Ian. *The New Orientalists: Postmodern Representations of Islam from Foucault to Baudrillard*. London: I.B. Tauris, 2007. Print.

Altaylı, Fatih. "Sevinsek Mi üzülsek Mi!" *Sabah*. N.p., 13 October 2006. Web. 10 September 2015. < http://arsiv.sabah.com.tr/2006/10/13/altayli.html>.

Amin, Samir. *Eurocentrism*. New York: Monthly Review, 2009. Print.

Anadolu-Okur, Nilgün. *Essays Interpreting the Writings of Novelist Orhan Pamuk: The Turkish Winner of the Nobel Prize in Literature*. Lampeter: Edwin Mellen, 2009. Print.

Arberry, A.J. *Classical Persian Literature*. London: George Allen and Unwin, 1958. Print.

Arslanoğlu, Kaan, Engin Yıldızoülu, Nihat Ateş, and Ali Mert. *5. Sanattan 5. Kola: Orhan Pamuk*. Istanbul: Ithaki, 2007. Print.

Attār, Farīd Al-Dīn and Margaret Smith. *The Persian Mystics: Attār*. New York: E.P. Dutton, 1932. Print.

——. *Pendname*. Trans. Yusuf Çetindağ. Istanbul: Etkileşim, 2013. Print.

Auerbach, Erich. *Mimesis: The Representation of Reality in Western Literature*. "Introduction" by Edward W. Said. Princeton, NJ: Princeton UP, 2003. Print.

Auster, Paul. *The New York Trilogy*. New York: Penguin, 2006. Print.

Bagheri, Mohammad Yusef. *Fifty Stories in English Poetry*. Tabriz: Forouzesh Publications, 2010. Print.

Balakrishnan, Gopal, ed. *Mapping the Nation*. "Introduction" by Benedict Anderson. Brooklyn, NY: Verso, 2012. Print.

Bassnett, Susan. *Comparative Literature: A Critical Introduction*. Oxford, UK: Blackwell, 1993. Print.

Bayer, Gamze Nur. *Orhan Pamuk'un "Cevdet Bey ve Oğulları" ile Thomas Mann'ın "Budden Brooks" Adlı Romanlarında Aile ve Toplum Eleştirisi*. Erzurum: Salkımsöğüt, 2012. Print.

Bednarz, Dieter and Volker Hage. "Frankfurt Book Fair Special: Orhan Pamuk and the Turkish Paradox." *Spiegel Online*. N.p., 21 October 2005. Web. 10 September 2015. <http://www.spiegel.de/international/spiegel/frankfurt-

book-fair-special-orhan-pamuk-and-the-turkish-paradox-a-380858-2.html>.

Belge, Murat. "Orhan Pamuk ve Murat Belge ile Nişantaşı Üzerine." *İstanbul Dergisi* 58 (2007). Print.

Blankley, Tony. *The West's Last Chance: Will We Win the Clash of Civilizations?* Washington, DC: Regnery Pub., 2005. Print.

Can, Şefik. *Fundamentals of Rumi's Thought: A Mevlevi Sufi Perspective*. Trans. Zeki Sarıtoprak. İzmir: Tughra, 2009. Print.

Carroll, Lewis. *Alice's Adventures in Wonderland*. New York: Samuel Gabriel Sons, 1916. Print. The Storyland Series.

Chiesa, Lorenzo. *Subjectivity and Otherness: A Philosophical Reading of Lacan*. London: Massachusetts Institute of Technology Press, 2007. Print.

Chua-Eoan, Howard. "The 2006 TIME 100." *Time*. Time Inc., 8 May 2006. Web. 04 Oct. 2015.
<http://content.time.com/time/specials/packages/article/0,28804,1975813_1975847_1976612,00.html>.

Clarke, J.J. *Jung and Eastern Thought: A Dialogue with the Orient*. London: Routledge, 1994. Print.

Cuddon, J.A. *The Penguin Dictionary of Literary Terms and Literary Theory*, 4th Edition. Ed. C.E. Preston. London: Penguin, 1999. Print.

Doğan, Zafer. *Orhan Pamuk Edebiyatında Tarih Ve Kimlik Söylemi*. Istanbul: İthaki, 2014. Print.

Dowlatabadi, Mahmoud. *Solook*. Tehran: Cheshme-Farhang-e Mo'aser, 2004. Print.

Dündar, Can, comp. "İşin Sırrı, Yazdığını Yırtıp Atabilmektir." *Milliyet* (15 October 2006), n.p. Web. 27 May 2014.
<http://www.milliyet.com.tr/2006/10/15/yazar/dundar.html>.

Eberstadt, Fernanda. "The Best Seller of Byzantium." *The New York Times*. The New York Times, (3 May 1997). Web. 8 September 2015.
<http://www.nytimes.com/1997/05/04/magazine/the-best-seller-of-byzantium.html?pagewanted=all>.

Ecevit, Yıldız. *Orhan Pamuk'u Okumak*. Vol. 9. Beyoğlu, İstanbul: Gerçek Yayınevi, 1996. Print.

Erol, Ahmet. *Turne Mektupları*. 3rd ed. Istanbul: YKY, 2008. Print.

Farman-Farmaian, Sattareh and Dona Munker. *Daughter of Persia: A Woman's Journey from Her Father's Harem through the Islamic Revolution*. New York: Three Rivers, 2006. Print.

Farrokh-Fal, Reza. *Hadise Ghorbat-e Sa'di* [*Sa'di's Roving Story*]. Tehran: Nashr-e Markaz, 2007. Print.

Ferdowsi, Abolghasem. *Shahnameh*. Tehran: Amirkabir, 1990. Print.

Firdawsī, and Reuben Levy. *The Epic of the Kings; Shah-nama, the National Epic of Persia*. Chicago: University of Chicago, 1967. Print.

Fukuyama, Francis. *The End of History and the Last Man*. New York: Avon, 1993. Print.

Genette, Gerard. *Palimpsests: Literature in the Second Degree.* Trans. Channa Newman and Claude Doubinsky. Vol. 8. Lincoln: University of Nebraska Press, 1997. Print. Stages.

Gökalp, Emre. "Pride and Anger: Orhan Pamuk's Nobel Prize and Discourses of Nationalism." *Anadolu University Journal of Social Sciences* 3rd ser. 10 (2007): 171-90. Web. 10 September 2015. < https://earsiv.anadolu.edu.tr/xmlui/bitstream/handle/11421/261/975842.pdf?sequence=1&isAllowed=y>.

Griffith, Ralph T.H. *Yusuf and Zulaikha: A Poem by Jami.* Routledge, 2013. Print.

Gündem, Mehmet. "Orhan Pamuk: 'Her Yazar Kendi Milletinin Kalbini Kazanmak Ister'" *Yeni Şafak* (23 Dec. 2006): n.p. Print.

Hadzibegovic, Darmin. *Kara Kitap'ın Sırları.* Istanbul: YKY, 2013. Print.

Halman, Talat Sait, ed. *Journal of Turkish Literature* 7. Orhan Pamuk Special Issue. Ankara: Syracuse University Press, 2010. Print.

——. *A Millennium of Turkish Literature: A Concise History.* Ed. Jayne L. Warner. Syracuse, NY: Syracuse University Press, 2011. Print.

Howard, Jane. *Inside Iran: Women's Lives.* Washington, DC: Mage, 2002. Print.

Ionesco, Eugène. *Rhinoceros; The Chairs; The Lesson.* Harmondsworth, Middlesex, England: Penguin, 1960. Print. Penguin Plays: 13.

Işık, Beril. *Aydınlıktan Karanlığa İktidar: Orhan Pamuk Romanlarında Demiryolu.* İstanbul: İletişim, 2012. Print.

Jameson, Fredric. *The Cultural Turn: Selected Writings on the Postmodern, 1983-1998.* London: Verso, 1998. Print.

Kamış, Mehmet. "Şehirler Ve Nobeller." *Zaman* (14 October 2006), n.p. Web. 10 September 2015. <http://www.zaman.com.tr/yazarlar/mehmet-kamis/sehirler-ve-nobeller_435222.html>.

Kılıc, Engin, ed. *Orhan Pamuk'u Anlamak.* İstanbul: İletişim, 1999. Print.

Lang, Andrew. *Tales from the Arabian Nights.* Hertfordshire: Wordsworth Editions, 1993. Print.

Lau, Jörg. "Struggling with the Elements of a Complicated History." *Qantara.de. Weekly Die Zeit,* 2005a. Web. 4 October 2015.

——. "The Turkish Trauma." *Signandsight.com. Die Zeit,* 14 April 2005b. Web. 4 October 2015. <http://www.signandsight.com/features/115.html>.

Lessing, Doris. *The Golden Notebook.* New York: Bantam, 1981. Print.

Levi-Strauss, Claude. *Tristes Tropiques.* Trans. John Russel. London: Hutchinson, 1961. Print.

Lyotard, Jean-Franc ois. *Lessons on the Analytic of the Sublime: Kant's Critique of Judgment, 23-29.* Stanford, CA: Stanford University Press, 1994. Print.

Mahammadi Asl, Abbas. *Jame'e Shenasi-e Max Weber [Max Weber's Sociology].* Tehran: Gol-Azin, 2011. Print.

Mani, B. Venkat. *Cosmopolitical Claims: Turkish-German Literatures from Nadolny to Pamuk.* Iowa City, IA: University of Iowa Press, 2007. Print.

Marien, Mary Warner. "Catch a Turkish Story Star." *Christian Science Monitor*, Vol. 83, No. 96 (12 April 1991), 13.

Márquez, Gabriel Garciá. *Love in the Time of Cholera*. Trans. Edith Grossman. Middlesex: Penguin, 1988. Print.

Matossian, Nouritza. "They Say 'incident'. To Me It's Genocide." *The Observer. The Guardian* (27 February 2005). Web. 10 September 2015. <http://www.theguardian.com/world/2005/feb/27/turkey.books>.

McGaha, Michael D. *Autobiographies of Orhan Pamuk: The Writer in His Novels*. Salt Lake City: University of Utah, 2008. Print.

Mernisi, Fatema. *Scheherazade Goes West: Different Cultures, Different Harems*. New York: Washington Square Press, 2001. Print.

Milani, Abbas. *Chand Goftar Darbareye Totalitarianism*. Tehran: Akhtaran, 2002. Print.

Mojaddedi, J.A. *The Biographical Tradition in Sufism: The Ṭabaqāt Genre from Al-Sulamī to Jāmī*. Richmond, Surrey: Curzon, 2001. Print.

Movahhed, Muhammad Ali. *Shams-e Tabrizi*. Tehran: Trh-e No, 2000. Print. Iran and Islamic Culture.

Munro, Alice. *Dear Life: Stories*. London: Vintage, 2013. Print.

Nizāmī, Ganjavī, and James Atkinson. *Laili' and Majnún: A Poem*. London: A.J. Valpy, publisher to the Oriental Translation Fund &c., 1836. Print.

Pamuk, Orhan. "An Honor for Turkish Literature." Interview by Dieter Bednarz. *Spiegel Online International*. N.p., (17 October 2006d). Web. 15 November 2015. <http://www.spiegel.de/international/interview-with-nobel-literature-prize-winner-orhan-pamuk-an-honor-for-turkish-literature-a-442928.html>.

——. *A Strangeness in My Mind*. Trans. Ekin Oklap. London: Faber and Faber, 2015. Print.

——. *Ben Bir Ağacım, Seçme Parçalar*. Istanbul: YKY, 2013a. Print.

——. *Gizli Yüz: Senaryo*. Istanbul: İletişim, 1993. Print.

——. *Kafamda Bir Tuhaflık*. Istanbul: YKY. 2014a. Print.

——. *Manzaradan Parçalar: Hayat, Sokaklar, Edebiyat*. İstanbul: İletişim, 2010a. Print.

——. "Memories of a Public Square." *The New Yorker*. N.p., 5 June 2013b. Web. 10 September 2015.

——. "Orhan Pamuk – Biographical." The Nobel Foundation, 2006c. Web. 19 September 2015. <http://www.nobelprize.org/nobel_prizes/literature/laureates/2006/pamuk-bio.html>.

——. "Orhan Pamuk: 'I Was Not A Political Person.'" Interview by Alexander Star. *The New York Times*, (14 August 2004a). Web. 15 November 2015. <http://www.nytimes.com/2004/08/15/books/interview-orhan-pamuk-i-was-not-a-political-person.html>.

——. "Orhan Pamuk: 'Les Bons Romans Doivent Révéler Au Monde Ce Qui Est Dissimulé Au Regard Ordinaire.'" Interview by Julien Bisson. *Lire* (July 2014b), 74-81. Print.

———. *Öteki Renkler: Seçme Yazılar Ve Bir Hikâye*. İstanbul: Yapı Kredi Yayınları, 2013c. Print.

———. *The Innocence of Objects: The Museum of Innocence*. Istanbul, New York: Abrams, 2012a. Print.

———. *The Museum of Innocence*. Trans. Maureen Freely. New York: Faber and Faber Limited, 2010b. Print.

———. "The Turkish Trauma." Interview by Jörg Lau. *Signandsight*. N.p., (18 April 2005b). Web. 15 November 2015. <http://www.signandsight.com/features/115.html>.

———. *Snow*. Trans. Maureen Freely. London: Faber and Faber, 2004b. Print.

Rypka, Jan. *History of Iranian Literature*. Ed. Karl Jahn. Vol. 5. Dordrecht: D. Reidel, 1968. Print.

Sa'di. *Golestan*. Intro. Mohammad Ali Foroughi. Tehran: Mojghan, 1994. Print.

———. *Bustan*. Intro. Mohammad Ali Foroughi.Tehran: Mojghan, 1994. Print.

Seval, Hale. *Orhan Pamuk ve Nakkaşlar*. Ankara: Ürün, 2015. Print.

Shafak, Elif. *The Forty Rules of Love*. London: Penguin, 2010. Print.

Solmaz, Yusuf. *Anlam Arayisi: Cevdet Bey ve Ogullari Romani Uzerine Bir Inceleme*. Vol. 1. N.p.: CreateSpace Independent Platform, 2011. Print.

Stone, Judy. "Orhan Pamuk: 'Enigma is Sovereign'" Editorial. *Publishers Weekly* (19 December 1994), 36+. *Orhan Pamuk Site*. Vol. 241, Issue 51, Trade Publication. Web. 4 Oct. 2015. <http://www.orhanpamuk.net/popuppage.aspx?id=68&lng=eng>.

Strath, Bo and Nina Witoszek. *The Postmodern Challenge: Perspectives East and West*. Amsterdam: Rodopi B.V., 1999. Print.

Todorov, Tzvetan. *French Literary Theory Today: A Reader*. Cambridge: Cambridge University Press, 1982. Print.

Vargas Llosa, M. Mario. *Chera Adabiyat?* [*Why Literature? Culture and Freedom*]. Trans. Abdollah Kosari. Tehran: Loh-e Fekr, 2005. Print.

Watson, Peter. *The Modern Mind: An Intellectual History of the 20th Century*. New York: HarperCollins, 2001. Print.

Wolfreys, Julian. *Introducing Criticism at the 21st Century*. Edinburgh: Edinburgh University Press, 2002. Print.

Worton, Michael and Judith Still. *Intertextuality: Theories and Practices*. Manchester: Manchester University Press, 1990. Print.

Yamanaka, Yuriko and Tetsuo Nishio. *The Arabian Nights and Orientalism: Perspectives from East and West*. Intro. R. Irwin. London: I.B. Tauris, 2006. Print.

Yazdanjoo, Payam. *Adabiyat-e Pasamodern* [*Postmodern Literature*]. Tehran: Markaz, 2001. Print.

Yüksel, Dilek Kuzulu. "5 Soruda Pamuk Davası." *Yeni Mesaj Gazetesi* (18 December 2005). Web. 16 April 2014. <http://www.yenimesaj.com.tr/?haber, 5020601>.

Zanganeh, Lila Azam. "Politics and Prose." *Columbia Magazine*. (2007) n.p. Web. 3 October 2015.

Index

A

Abdulrahman Munif, 57
Abu Said abol-Khayr, 93
academic, 20, 28, 34, 106
adventure, x, 58
Afghanistan, 91, 99, 102
Afrasiyab, 88
Africa, vii, 21, 34
African, 3
Ahmad Ghazali, x
Ahmet Hamdi Tanpınar, 7, 50, 63
Ahmet Ümit, 7
Aimé Césaire, 5
Alaaddin, 90, 96
Alaturka, 62
Alexander the Great, 102
Al-Ghazali, 85, 92
Ali Shariati, 33
alienation, viii, 78, 111
Ali-Shir Nava'i, 82, 91, 93
allegory, 74
allusion, 74
Al-sīra al-Nabawiyya, 87
America, 3, 27, 45, 102, 107, 124, 125, 128
American, vii, viii, 18, 27, 62, 99, 101, 102, 105, 124, 126
Americans, 49, 66, 101, 102
Amir Khosrow, 91
anachronistic, 76
analogy, 37
anarchy, 106
Anatolian, 103, 116, 119
anatomy, 46
ancestry, 46
ancient, x, 10, 15, 18, 30, 34, 45, 67, 79, 92, 116
André Gide, 50
anecdotes, 94
angel, 92
antagonism, 19
Anthony Appiah, 10, 15, 31, 37, 46, 115
anthropology, 12, 31, 39, 43
antiphilosophy, 92
antiquity, ix, 44
antithesis, 14
Antoine Galland, 89, 90
apotheosis, 6
approach, xi, 17, 53, 68, 104, 108, 117
Arab, 18, 21, 45, 82, 87, 89, 90, 109, 116
Arabian Nights, x, *89*, *131*, *133*
Arabic, ix, 51, 57, 61, 81, 85, 86, 89, 90, 91, 92, 96, 119
Arabicized, 57
Arabist, 89
archetypes, 77
architecture, 33
Architextuality, 73
Aristotelian, 66
Aristotle, 37, 110
Armenia, 84
Armenian, 83
article, 69, 71, 98, 109, 124, 125, 130
artist, 33, 83
artistic, 28, 74, 101, 109
arts, 33, 80
assimilation, 39, 67, 114
Attar, x, 77, 85, 93, 128

Auerbach, 110, 129
Australia, 27, 102
author, vii, viii, ix, x, 7, 50, 66, 67, 69, 71, 75, 76, 86, 103, 104, 108, 110, 111, 117, 119, 120
autobiography, 99
autonomy, 31, 55, 75
avant-garde, 77
avatars, 114
Azade Seyhan, viii, 50
Azar Nafisi, 99, 102
Azerbaijan, 82
Azeri, 81

B

Baba Taher, 82
Bafqi, 84
Baghdad, 85, 87
Bakhtin, xi, 67, 68, 69, 123
Barthes, xi, 39, 67, 69, 70, 71, 72, 73, 111, 123
Baudrillard, 108, 129
Bayezid II, 92
Benedict Anderson, 5, 36, 37, 46, 48, 107, 129
Bernard Lewis, 35, 45
Bertolt Brecht, 111
bestseller, 99, 100, 102, 105, 118, 120
Beyoğlu, 103, 130
biography, 71, 87
Bosphorus, 6, 102, 119
boundaries, 31, 47, 58, 66
Britain, 99, 100, 120
British, 1, 4, 46, 89
Buddhism, 13, 115
Bulgarian, 67
bureaucracy, 48
Bustan, x, 85, 133

C

Caliphate, 85
Calvino, 79
Cambridge, 86, 123, 124, 125, 126, 127, 133
Cannes, 102
capitalism, 10, 22, 26, 27, 29, 102
catastrophe, 68
Cevdet Bey and His Sons, 116
Chalabi, 94, 97
chaos, 10
chaotic, 7
China, 34, 112
Chinese, 34, 98
Chivalric, 65
cholera, 33
Christian, 3, 16, 27, 89, 90, 115, 120, 132
chronologies, 55
churches, 27
Circassians, 49
civilization, x, 1, 2, 3, 16, 20, 25, 28, 29, 33, 35, 45, 49, 54, 106, 114, 121
Classical, 14, 28, 60, 67, 81, 129
cliché, 51
Colin Campbell, xi, 1, 113
colonialism, 22, 42, 43, 49, 120
colonization, 34, 49, 105, 114
colonized, 3, 5, 18, 43, 57
comparatists, 11, 28, 55
comparative literature, xi, 11, 53, 54, 55, 56, 81, 100, 109, 120
comparativism, 56
conspiracy, 19
context, xi, 4, 6, 10, 19, 39, 43, 44, 66, 70, 74, 77, 78, 100, 104, 107, 108, 110, 111, 120
contextualization, 107
contexture, 71
cosmology, 66

cosmopolitan, 4, 7, 29, 50, 85, 104, 115
cosmopolitanism, 4, 32, 110, 120
couplets, x
Critical, 26, 129
criticism, 26, 69, 71, 102, 110
criticize, 20, 28
critics, 50, 60, 67, 74, 75, 97, 100, 104, 119
critique, 27, 43, 54
cross-cultural, 9, 31, 56
customs, 4, 12, 44
Czesław Miłosz, 28

D

Dadaist, 112
Damascus, 96
Damrosch, xi, 53, 55, 81, 104, 117, 118, 120, 124
Daniel Defoe, 86
Dante, 79
Darwin, 15
David Damrosch, 54
Decameron, 79
decapitation, 88
decolonization, 105, 119
decontextualization, 107
democracy, 58, 103
democratic, 29, 103
demythologize, 19
de-Orientalize, 19, 23
depersonalization, 14
Derrida, 28, 39, 69, 76, 109, 110, 124
dervish, 93, 95, 96
de-Westernization, 2
dialectical, 39, 77
dichotomous, 29
didactic, 81, 100
Différance, 109
Diwan-e Shams-e Tabrizi, 98

Diyar-ı Kalp, 79
dogmatic, 5, 28, 105, 119, 120
Dostoyevsky, 75, 106
dualism, 9
Dublin, 104
duplication, 59

E

Easterner, 32, 33, 38, 111, 115
Easternization, i, xi, 1, 2, 3, 4, 5, 6, 9, 10, 13, 16, 17, 18, 19, 25, 26, 28, 29, 31, 33, 39, 40, 47, 48, 53, 55, 61, 65, 81, 85, 99, 101, 102, 103, 104, 105, 106, 107, 111, 113, 114, 115, 116, 117, 118, 119, 120, 123, 124
Easternized, 2, 25
Eastern-oriented, 65, 99, 113, 115, 118, 120
Eastern-style, 9, 13, 115
Eastern-world, 34
East-West, 9, 45, 56, 77, 106, 112, 116, 117, 125
Eclecticism, 13
ecumenicalism, 19
Edward Said, xi, 10, 11, 17, 18, 20, 21, 27, 29, 34, 35, 46, 54, 57, 59, 60, 74, 105, 108, 116, 128
ego, 42, 52, 59, 108
Egypt, 90
Egyptian, 90, 99
Elif Şafak, 63
elucidating, 5, 22
English, x, 61, 75, 89, 104, 118, 129
enigma, 71
Erdağ Göknar, 104, 118
Esfandyar, 87
ethical, 13
ethics, ix
Eurocentric, 3, 5, 10, 20, 28, 43, 54, 56, 57, 101, 105, 106, 119, 120

Eurocentricism, 54
exceptionalism, 5
Exoticism, 59, 109

F

faith, 25, 50, 92
fang shui, 115
fantastic, x, 35, 59, 62, 65, 101
Farsi, 81, 85, 86, 92, 93, 104, 118
fatalism, 36
father, x, 82, 83, 84, 88, 91, 95
Ferdowsi, ix, x, 83, 85, 86, 88, 125, 130
fiqh, 92
Firoozeh Dumas, 99
francophone, 56
Frankfurt, 78, 103, 129
Frantz Fanon, 42, 57
Fredric Jameson, 10, 111, 125
French, 10, 46, 47, 59, 67, 89, 93, 133
Freud, 51, 69, 75, 124, 125
Freudian, 16
Friedrich Nietzsche, 9
fundamentalism, 11
Fuzûlî, 81

G

Gabriel Garcia Marquez, ix
gender, 107
genealogy, 34
Genette, 73, 131
genocide, 103
George W. Bush, vii, 58, 102
German, 1, 59, 131
Germany, vii, 78, 104, 120, 127
Ghazali, x, 92, 93, 98
Ghazni, 87
globalism, 35

globalization, ix, 3, 6, 17, 27, 55, 115
god, 3
Goethe, 29, 53, 59, 86, 104, 117, 118
Greece, 30, 60, 120
Greek, 33, 47, 69, 87, 100, 117
Gulistan, 85
Gulliver's Travels, 59

H

Hafiz, 82
Haft Awrang, x, 91
Halide Edib, 22, 31, 46, 49, 57
Halit Ziya Uşaklıgil, 63
Hamlet, 75
Hanif Kureishi, 99
Hannah Arendt, 4
Harold Bloom, 75, 76
Haruki Murakami, 99
Harun al-Rashid, 89
Hebrews, 15
hedonism, 86
Hegel, 14, 39
Hegelian, 39, 44
hegemony, 6, 11, 18, 22, 28
Hellenistic, 33
hermeneutics, 4, 9, 65
hierarchy, 61
Hinduism, 13
homeland, 61
Homer, 21, 66, 88
Homeric, 15
Homi Bhabha, 4, 11, 32, 42
homoerotic, ix
homogeneous, 12
homology, 55
Hüsn ü Aşk, 79
Hüsrev and Shirin, 84
Hüzün, 50, 51, 103, 120
hybridity, 11, 46, 55, 100

hypertextuality, 73
hypothetical, 10, 36

I

ideology, 46, 106, 107
imitate, 36, 50, 61
imitating, 48, 57, 75, 114
imitation, 15, 28, 33, 47, 48, 61, 62, 65, 68, 70, 74, 75, 91, 110, 111
immigration, 105
immortality, 94
imperialism, 22, 46
imperialist, 21
individualism, 16, 22, 25, 46, 92
individualistic, 25, 92
industrialism, 29
information, 11, 15, 107
injustice, x, 75
innate, 16, 110
inner, 20, 29, 31, 32, 49, 77, 90, 116, 118
intellectual, viii, 2, 10, 18, 19, 20, 26, 28, 60, 77, 105, 116
intertext, 70, 71, 72, 73, 76
intertextuality, xi, 7, 12, 53, 65, 66, 67, 69, 70, 71, 72, 73, 74, 75, 76, 77, 78, 81, 85, 105, 109, 111, 112, 113, 118, 119
irony, 27, 74, 86, 111
irrationality, 19
Isaiah Berlin, 37
isolation, viii, 107
İstanbul, viii, 102, 103, 104, 119, 120, 123, 124, 126, 129, 130, 131, 132

J

Jalal Al-Ahmed, 33
Jami, x, 82, 85, 91, 131
Jewish, 120

Joseph and Zulaikha, 91
Judaism, 3, 19
Jung, 15, 125, 130
justice, 89

K

Kadıköy, 103
Kafka, ix, 79
Kalila and Dimna, x
Kant, 15, 39, 131
Kanuni, 75
Kars, 103
Kazuo Ishiguro, 99
Kelile and Dimne, 80, 90, 92
Kemal Tahir, 7
Kemalist, 35
Khaled Hosseini, 99
Khatami, 5, 101
Khausrau Parviz, x
Khorasan, 91
Khosrow and Shirin, 82, 83, 84, 85, 86, 91, 93
Khusrau and Shirin, x
king Shahryar, x
Konya, 95, 96
Koran, 51
Krishna, 13, 115
Kristeva, xi, 67, 68, 69, 70, 71, 72, 73, 125
Kyd, 75

L

Lacan, 42, 59, 69, 125, 130
Lacanian, 42
language, ix, 23, 37, 45, 54, 55, 57, 61, 66, 68, 70, 79, 86, 89, 94, 97, 104, 107, 108, 111, 120
Layla and Majnun, 82, 85, 91
Lévi-Strauss, 51, 69
Leyla and Mejnun, 83

liberalism, 11, 32, 120
lifestyle, 50, 120
linguistic, 44, 46, 55, 56, 67, 111
literacy, 57
literal, 14, 73
literary, vii, viii, ix, x, xi, 6, 20, 26, 27, 34, 45, 53, 54, 55, 61, 62, 65, 67, 68, 69, 72, 73, 74, 76, 77, 78, 81, 85, 87, 94, 99, 100, 101, 102, 104, 105, 106, 107, 110, 112, 113, 115, 116, 117, 118, 119, 120
literature, vii, viii, ix, x, xi, 7, 22, 27, 29, 44, 50, 53, 54, 55, 56, 58, 59, 62, 65, 66, 67, 69, 72, 74, 76, 77, 78, 80, 81, 85, 89, 91, 92, 99, 100, 101, 102, 103, 104, 105, 107, 110, 111, 113, 114, 117, 118, 119, 120, 132
logocentrism, 28
logoteunison, 65, 113
London, 99, 100, 123, 125, 126, 127, 128, 129, 130, 131, 132, 133
love, x, 22, 27, 36, 79, 81, 82, 83, 84, 85, 88, 94, 95, 96, 97, 106, 109
Lyotard, 26, 109, 110, 120, 131

M

Mahnaz Afridi, 60
Majnun, x, 82, 83, 85, 91
manifest, 79, 104
manifestation, 49
manifesto, 68, 78
Mann, 78, 79, 129
Mansur Hallaj, x
Mario Levi, 7
Marxism, 26, 33, 102
masterpieces, x, xi, 53, 65, 78, 81, 85, 101, 105, 107, 112, 117, 118, 119, 120
materialism, 16, 31, 33, 101, 115
Mathnawi, 80, 94, 95, 97, 98

Matthew Arnold, 86
Maureen Freely, 118, 126, 127, 133
Mediterranean, 47, 48
memoir, 51, 77
memoirist, 102
metalanguage, 68
metanarrative, 26, 77, 109
metaphor, 102, 106, 119
metaphysical, 9, 16, 115
Metatextuality, 73
meter, ix
methodological, 68, 70
methodology, 17
Mevlevi, 75, 130
Michael Riffaterre, 68
Michel Foucault, 69, 110
Middle-East, 18, 58
migration, 55
Miguel de Cervantes, 59
mimesis, 74, 76, 105, 110
mimicry, 42, 59, 111
miniature, ix
miniaturist, 84, 87
modernist, 3, 76
modernity, 3, 18, 23, 25, 26, 34, 35, 116
modernization, 3, 9, 26, 28, 34, 35, 36, 49
Mongols, 45
monism, 9, 16, 115
monopolizing, 17
monotonic, 76
morality, 9, 85, 90
multiculturalism, 4, 11, 12, 27, 31, 108, 115
multi-ethnic, 7
multilingual, vii, 7, 28
multinational, vii, 27
multiplicity, 10, 71, 109
multipolar, 54
Muslim, 18, 42, 45, 47, 48, 57, 92

mystic, ix, 29, 84, 92, 94, 97, 102, 104, 117
mysticism, 13, 92, 93, 98, 120
myth, 13, 59, 115
mythology, ix, 67, 87, 90

N

Nadr ibn al-Harith, 87
Naguib Mahfouz, 99
Nahid Rachlin, 99
Nâilî, 81
narcissistic, 16
Nasr Allah Munshi, 93
nationalism, 5, 18, 28, 31, 34, 45, 46, 47, 54, 56, 59, 103, 104
nationalist, 11, 44, 46
nationalistic, 47, 109
nationality, 46, 86, 100, 107
nationhood, 31
nation-states, 4, 54
NATO, 120
naturalization, 46
Nedim Gürsel, 7
New York Trilogy, 79, 129
nineteenth century, 6, 15
Nizami, ix, x, 82, 83, 84, 85, 91, 98
nonconscious, 39
nondiscriminatory, 84
non-European, 28, 53, 54
non-fiction, vii, 81, 100, 119
non-identity, 39
nonmanipulative, 18
non-Western, 17, 18, 28, 31, 32, 34, 43, 53, 56, 57, 59, 61
norm, 108
novelist, viii, 58, 60, 111, 115, 119
novelty, 14, 32
Nuruddin Farah, 99

O

Occidental, 36, 44, 48
Oedipus, 75
Oğuz Atay, 63
Orhan Pamuk, i, vii, 6, 62, 74, 99, 100, 101, 102, 103, 105, 113, 119, 120, 123, 124, 125, 126, 128, 129, 130, 131, 132, 133
Orientalism, xi, 3, 17, 18, 19, 20, 21, 22, 34, 35, 43, 59, 60, 105, 106, 109, 116, 121, 124, 125, 127, 128, 133
Orientalist, 18, 19, 20, 21, 22, 39, 82, 92, 109, 120
Orientalizing, 23
Orient-versus-Occident, 21
otherness, 18, 19, 21, 27, 39, 42, 43, 44, 57, 109
Ottoman, vii, ix, 7, 23, 34, 40, 45, 48, 49, 52, 62, 77, 80, 81, 89, 92, 93, 103, 112, 119, 120
Ottoman dynasty, 103

P

Pakistan, 93, 99
parable, x, 97
paradigm, 29, 33, 66
paradise, 35, 86
paradoxical, 100
paratextuality, 73
Parisianization, 110
parochialism, 31
parody, 27, 53, 71, 73, 74, 76, 111
Pascale Casanova, 54, 107
past, viii, ix, 7, 9, 17, 23, 27, 37, 40, 43, 45, 46, 48, 50, 52, 54, 58, 61, 62, 75, 77, 105, 120
pastiche, xi, 53, 65, 74, 76, 78, 105, 111, 118
Paul Auster, ix, 79, 119

peace, 31, 106
pedagogy, 54
perplexity, 12
Persia, 15, 33, 130
Persian, ix, x, 29, 33, 57, 59, 78, 81, 82, 85, 86, 88, 92, 93, 94, 97, 104, 119, 123, 128, 129
phenomenal, 42
phoenix, 88
Plato, 32, 66, 110
Platonic, 66
Plotinus, 41
pluralism, 31
plurality, 70
polarities, 12, 39
polyphony, 67, 68, 72
polytheism, 18
postindustrial, 25
postmodernism, xi, 25, 26, 27, 41, 67, 74, 76, 105, 116, 118
postmodernity, 4, 10, 26, 27
Postmodernization, 27
post-occidentalism, 18
Post-Orientalism, 18
post-structuralism, 67, 71
post-Western, 25, 115
pre-modern, 92
pre-texts, 65
Progressivism, 26
Protestantism, 10
provincialism, 54
psychological, 16
psychology, 15, 69, 71
Pythagoras, 41

Q

Qays, 82
Quinary, 82, 83
Quran, x, 91, 94, 97

R

racial, 22
radical, 12, 16, 29
rationalism, 10
rationality, 9, 10, 19
rationalization, 10, 13, 26, 102, 113, 116, 118
realism, 32, 104, 119
realistic, 5, 60, 62, 76, 111
reasoning, 99, 117
rebellious, 18
relativism, 9, 12, 27, 59
religion, 3, 13, 23, 27, 30, 35, 37, 41, 85, 103, 107, 115, 120
religious, 3, 7, 9, 11, 13, 37, 50, 88, 92, 105, 114, 115
Renaissance, 34, 44, 85
Republic, ix, 40, 110, 124
Republican, 23, 49, 77
rhetoric, 12
rhyme, ix
rivalry, 88, 101, 103
Robinson Crusoe, 59, 86
romanticism, 58
Rostam, x, 87, 88
Rudaki, 82
Rumi, x, 41, 42, 58, 77, 79, 82, 85, 94, 95, 96, 97, 98, 103, 118, 123, 130

S

Sa'di, 82, 85, 93, 128, 130, 133
Samuel P. Huntington, 5
Sander L. Gilman, vii
Sanskrit, 90, 92, 119
Sassanid, 86, 89, 93
Sassanid dynasty, 86, 89
Satan, 88
Satareh Farman Farmaian, 99
satiric, 111

Saussurian, 67
Scheherazade, x, 89, 90, 132
Schopenhauer, 15
secularism, ix, 77, 103, 120
secularization, 13, 17
self-appointed, 43
self-awareness, 27
self-colonization, 49
self-confidence, 48
self-consciousness, 20, 36
self-contained, 9, 14, 114
self-deception, 95
self-defined, 20
self-deification, 16
self-esteem, 94
self-evident, 108
self-help, 101, 117
self-identity, 20, 35
self-imposed, 23
Self-knowledge, 96
self-realization, 33
self-reflexive, 27
self-reliance, 16
self-representation, 18
self-secularization, 13
self-study, 2, 114
self-sufficient, 67
self-termed, 37
Semiotic, 125
sexual, 96, 97
Seyyed Hossein Nasr, 29, 126
Shahnameh, x, 86, 88, 125, 130
Shakespeare, 75, 82, 100
shamanism, 15
Shams al-Din of Tabriz, x
Shams of Tabriz, 95, 96, 97, 98, 103
Shams-e Tabrizi, 98, 132
Shirvanshah, 82
signified, 44, 69
signifiers, 69
signify, 66, 72
simulacrum, 35

Simurgh, 87, 94
Şişli, 103
Siyavush, 88
slave, 40, 41, 77, 89, 97
slavery, 9
sociality, 34
socio-cultural, 1
socio-economic, 34
socio-global, 19
sociological, xi
sociologist, xi, 33, 67
Sohrab and Rustum, 86
Somalia, 99
Sonnets, 94
Sophocles, 75
spiritualism, 120
structuralism, 67, 71, 73
subcultures, 1, 113
Sufi, ix, 29, 41, 42, 77, 81, 85, 91, 93, 94, 123, 130
Sufism, x, xi, 13, 15, 65, 77, 81, 92, 96, 115, 119, 120, 132
Sultan, 83, 92, 93, 98
supranationality, 56
surah, x
Swiss, 103
symbolic, 39, 42, 44
symbolism, 15
symbolize, 52
symbolized, 117
symbols, vii, x, 1, 45
synthesis, 62
Syria, 90, 102
Syrian, 89, 104

T

t'ai chi, 13, 115
Taha Neda, 81
Talât Halman, 45, 58, 62, 106
Tanzimat, 35, 49, 62, 100
technologization, 14

The binary opposition, 52
The Epic of Kings, x, 83, 84
The Great Divan, 95, 98
The Naïve and the Sentimental Novelist, viii, 117
The Orchard, 85
The Rubaiyat of Omar Khayyam, 105
the Swedish Academy, vii, 106
The Timurid dynasty, 102
the United Kingdom, 15
theism, 117
thematic, 81
theme, vii, 7, 14, 22, 35, 45, 74, 76, 77, 79, 120
theology, 16, 92, 115
theosophy, 29
thesis, xi, 2, 6, 10, 13, 16, 17, 25, 26, 29, 33, 53, 55, 85, 99, 102, 105, 113, 116, 119, 120
Timurid, 91, 102
Titans, 87
Todorov, 5, 101, 108, 128, 133
tragedy, x, 28, 73
transcultural, 12
trans-European, 28
trans-historical, 10
transposition, 33, 73, 74
transtextuality, 73
travesty, 74
Tristes Tropiques, 51, 131
Tristesse, 51, 120
Turanian, 87, 88
Turkey, vii, viii, ix, 6, 35, 40, 45, 47, 48, 49, 50, 58, 60, 62, 74, 78, 94, 100, 103, 104, 112, 114, 116, 120, 124
Türkic, 87
Turkicised, 49
Turkish, vii, viii, ix, 6, 7, 27, 31, 45, 47, 48, 49, 50, 51, 62, 74, 75, 77, 80, 81, 90, 92, 93, 101, 103, 105, 112, 119, 124, 125, 128, 129, 131, 132, 133
Turkishness, 7
twelfth-century, 94
twenty-first century, viii, 55

U

Umberto Eco, 75, 119
uncivilized, 4
UNESCO, 87
universalism, 5, 35
universalization, 110
urbanization, 26
Utopianism, 12

V

V.S. Naipaul, 57
Vahshi Bafqi, 84
Vargas Llosa, 111, 128, 133
Voltaire, 86

W

Weber, xi, 1, 3, 9, 10, 13, 106, 110, 113, 114, 128, 131
Weberian, xi, 1, 3, 4, 9, 10, 13, 102, 113, 118
Weltanschauung, ix, 1
Weltliteratur, 53
West-Central, 14
Westernization, ix, 2, 4, 6, 17, 19, 28, 29, 32, 33, 35, 47, 48, 101, 105, 114, 115, 121
Westernized, 49, 114
Western-style, 33, 35, 65, 99, 104, 109, 119
Westoccification, 33
West-struck-ness, 33

X

xenophobia, 11

Y

Yaşar Kemal, 62

Yusuf and Zulaikha, x, 131

Z

Zarrinkoob, 91, 128
Zen, 13, 115
Zülfü Livaneli, 7, 63